SEA SALT

RECIPES *from the* WEST COAST GALLEY

SEA SALT

ALISON MALONE EATHORNE, HILARY MALONE & LORNA MALONE

HARBOUR

Harbour Publishing Co. Ltd.
P.O. Box 219, Madeira Park, BC, V0N 2H0
www.harbourpublishing.com

Food Styling—Hilary Malone and Christina Symons
Editor—Pam Robertson
Cover and text design—Five Seventeen/Picapica.ca
Indexer—Iva Cheung

Additional Photo Credits:
Page 21: 'Fresh Fish Market, Sidney.' ALISON MALONE EATHORNE PHOTO. Page 34:
'Apple tree branch.' THINKSTOCK PHOTO. Page 61: 'Candied salmon.' THINKSTOCK
PHOTO. Page 92: 'Dried mushrooms.' HILARY MALONE PHOTO. Page 165: 'Clams.'
HILARY MALONE PHOTO. Page 180: 'Boots.' DAVE HEATH PHOTO. Page 198:
'Winch.' TESSA KENNING PHOTO. Page 209: 'Racing deck.' DAVE HEATH PHOTO.

Printed on chlorine-free paper made with 10% post-consumer waste

Printed and bound in Canada

Canada Council
for the Arts

Conseil des Arts
du Canada

BRITISH
COLUMBIA
ARTS COUNCIL
Supported by the Province of British Columbia

Harbour Publishing acknowledges financial support from the Government of
Canada through the Canada Book Fund and the Canada Council for the Arts,
and from the Province of British Columbia through the BC Arts Council and the
Book Publishing Tax Credit.

LIBRARY AND ARCHIVES CANADA CATALOGUING IN PUBLICATION

Eathorne, Alison Malone
    Sea salt : recipes from the west coast galley / Alison Malone
Eathorne, Hilary Malone & Lorna Malone.
Includes index.

ISBN 978-1-55017-555-4

    1. Cooking, Canadian—British Columbia style. 2. Cooking—
British Columbia—Vancouver Island. 3. Cookbooks. I. Malone,
Hilary II. Malone, Lorna III. Title.

TX715.6.E24 2013   641.59711'2   C2013-900210-3

Aeriel manoeuvres on the start line of the Van Isle 360.
DAVE HEATH PHOTO

For Adeline Hawken, Lorna's mother, who greeted entertaining and creativity in the kitchen with gusto

For Irene Malone, Alison and Hilary's paternal grandmother, for teaching us the importance of gathering around the family dinner table

For Liam Eathorne, Alison's son, the most recent addition to our crew

CONTENTS

Introduction

Sea Salt invites you on a culinary adventure around Vancouver Island. It's a voyage that can be shared by all of us who enjoy cooking and eating local, seasonal food in a spectacular environment.

Vancouver Island and the many islands off its eastern shores are world renowned as a cruising destination. Boaters are drawn to the rugged coastline, snow-capped mountains, unspoiled beaches, protected anchorages and the rich biological diversity of our region.

While travelling these waters, sailors are exposed to many areas of culinary interest, including the Saanich Peninsula, the Cowichan Valley, Salt Spring Island,

Cortes Island and the more remote northern reaches of Vancouver Island. These areas are home to fine-food artisans, growers, farmers' markets, wineries and cideries that are acclaimed for their high-quality products. *Sea Salt*'s recipes will highlight these ingredients and the producers responsible for them. We encourage you to source and utilize local food and make it an exciting part of your coastal cruising experience.

My sailing experience began on Lake Huron after my husband and I acquired a small cruising sailboat, while living in Ontario. Some years later, I had the opportunity to sail with Haydn and Sylvia Gozzard

Wing on wing, *Aeriel* heads for Texada Island. ALISON MALONE EATHORNE PHOTO

Alison enjoys a summer day in the cockpit, Victoria Harbour, *circa* 1990.

Lorna with her well-fed racing crew, 2001. PHOTOS COURTESY LORNA MALONE

on *Renegade* during the Port Huron to Mackinac Race. The demanding 470-km (300-mi) course gave me my first appreciation of the importance of food preparation for an extended voyage. The *Renegade* crew enjoyed the warm, hearty food that Sylvia had prepared in advance, which helped us keep pushing to what would be an excellent finish in our division.

Bill and I left our boat behind when we moved to Nanaimo in the late 1970s. The next ten years were an exciting and busy time with our three children. We would wait a decade before owning another boat, and this time it would be *Aeriel*, a McCurdy & Rhodes design, built for us by Bent Jespersen and his talented crew in Sidney. *Aeriel* is a beautiful wooden boat, as magnificent today as she was 23 years ago when she first settled into the water behind Bent's shop. I write this having just returned from another sunny, warm week cruising the Gulf Islands on *Aeriel*.

Our early days were spent sailing our local waters with our small children, Alison, Ryan and Hilary—aged eight, six and two when *Aeriel* was launched in 1989. As the children grew older, we enjoyed preparing meals together. Alison often looked after lunch, creating her daily specials and passing them out through the quarter-berth window to her customers in the cockpit—simple food and great entertainment.

Our racing experience with *Aeriel* has included numerous Swiftsure and Southern Straits races, as well as the Van Isle 360 International Yacht Race, a two-week circumnavigation of Vancouver Island. Planning meals for eight crew members in a race of this duration was a challenging task. There were many factors to take into consideration and my plan was always to prepare much of the food in advance. However, I also strove to serve fresh food, when possible, to create variety and interest. By our fourth Van Isle 360, I think I had it about right, whether it was preparing breakfast on our way to an early start or passing out a hot, one-bowl meal to the crew at midnight while running down the island's west coast.

Over the years, I have become increasingly aware of the tremendous variety of locally grown produce, meat, dairy products and of course seafood available on Vancouver Island, the Gulf Islands and the Discovery Islands. I enjoy the excitement and satisfaction that comes with sourcing local ingredients and products wherever we are cruising. When combined with a well-stocked pantry, local food provides endless possibilities for creative cooking.

Our children, now adults, love to cook. Trialling countless recipes over the years with Alison and Hilary has resulted in this book. Scallops, lamb, blueberries,

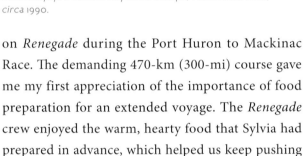

OPPOSITE PAGE, CLOCKWISE FROM TOP: *Aeriel* was built in 1989. A summer sail in gentle breezes, Nanaimo Harbour. TERRY PATTERSON PHOTO. Hilary at the helm, 1994. TERRY PATTERSON PHOTO. Family fun on the aft deck, 1994. PHOTO COURTESY LORNA MALONE. *Aeriel* sailing off Saanich Penninsula with Mount Baker in view, 2001. KELLY O'NEIL PHOTO

Bill Malone and Hilary's basil soak up the sun aboard *Aeriel*.

indicate throughout this collection the recipes best suited to being made in advance of your trip.

Chapter one, Breakaway, rewards the first night of your journey with the freshest of ingredients while the second chapter, Brunch, captures the magic of a leisurely morning in one of your favourite anchorages. Chapter three, On the Beach, puts you ashore with the perfect picnic. Fresh, chapter four, will help you celebrate the days spent sourcing local food, whether it's perusing produce at a farmers' market or plucking seafood from your trap or fishing line. The next chapter, Entertaining: On the Dock and Rafting Up, showcases simple appetizers, dinner ideas and desserts well suited to sharing with fellow boaters when it's your turn to host.

North, chapter six, offers dishes that utilize ingredients with a longer shelf life, including hardy fruits and vegetables, as well as pantry staples. Chapter seven, Racing, brings together soul-satisfying dishes that are guaranteed to sustain the morale of your crew. The final chapter, Condiments, Etc., is a list of delicious accompaniments that can be made at home or on board.

Boating around Vancouver Island provides many opportunities for memorable cooking and eating experiences. Our hope is to help you make such experiences possible by illustrating the benefits of thoughtful preparation, smart storage strategies, clever shortcuts and a hearty dose of creativity. We encourage you to source and utilize coastal ingredients, whether they come from a grocery store, a farmers' market, an independent food store or your own fishing rod. *Sea Salt* has been created for you, the boater who loves to cook and wishes to produce the same high-quality fare in your galley as you do at home. You will enjoy wonderful food and have great fun!

—Lorna Malone

hazelnuts and wild mushrooms are just a few of the coastal ingredients we have used in our recipes, and represent a small fraction of what is available to us. It would take more than one cookbook to fully showcase the local bounty we enjoy. While we have created the recipes using our favourite ingredients, we encourage you to be creative and make substitutions based on what is fresh and available to you.

The first section of the book is our Toolbox, a list of kitchen tools and equipment that we don't leave port without. In The Galley Pantry you will find our list of pantry and refrigerator staples that we keep stocked in the galley, as well as helpful tips for on-board food storage. And Planning Ahead outlines how we

The Toolbox

Galley kitchens are inherently smaller than home kitchens and don't have the space for an extensive supply of tools, gadgets, small appliances and ingredients. This section provides our list of essential hand tools—many of which serve numerous purposes—along with our go-to list of pantry and refrigerator staples we stock before every journey at sea.

KITCHEN TOOLS

A sturdy 8- by 12-in (20- by 30-cm) plastic container with a tight-fitting lid will hold most of the hand tools you will need in your galley. These items include:

- bottle opener
- can opener
- medium Microplane grater
- soup ladle
- potato masher
- measuring spoons
- metal spatula
- silicone spatula
- scissors
- tongs
- vegetable peeler
- whisk
- wooden spoon
- packet of wooden skewers (for the barbecue)
- oyster shucker
- crab shell cracker
- salt and pepper grinders

IN ADDITION TO THIS LIST, YOU WILL NEED:

- large chef's knife (for chopping)
- serrated knife (for bread and delicate produce)
- small paring knife
- set of nesting measuring cups
- 2 nesting stainless steel mixing bowls (which can do double duty as serving bowls)
- serving tray(s)
- 2 chopping boards (at least 1 synthetic to use when handling meat products)
- parchment paper
- heavy-strength aluminium foil (for cooking on the barbecue)
- colander (collapsible, if available)
- large stockpot (for live crab, or soups and stews when cooking for a crowd)
- 2 saucepans (medium and small)
- large, deep-sided, non-stick sauté pan with lid (ideal for one-dish meals)
- medium non-stick or stainless steel sauté pan
- rectangular roast pan
- rimmed baking sheet
- either 8-in (20-cm) or 9-in (23-cm) square baking pan

Before purchasing these items, measure the size of your burner on your stove and the inside dimensions of your oven to ensure that the pans you purchase are not too large.

Hilary pops up from the galley off Newcastle Island.

Many of us have one more item that we feel we can't live without in the galley. If you have a tool that makes your cooking more enjoyable and you have the storage space, consider adding it. For us, this item is a hand-held immersion blender with a bowl attachment, which can blend, whisk, whip and chop. It goes directly in the soup pot for a lovely purée and can whip up a silky smooth hummus in no time when friends raft up for appetizers and drinks. It is great for sauces, smoothies and salad dressings, too. There are cordless models available but they do require recharging. We use a standard, 120-volt model plugged into an inverter when shore power is not available.

The Galley Pantry

Stocking a galley can be a challenge. Storage space, heat sources and refrigeration—as well as the nature of your boating adventure, destination and duration—all play a hand in what you stock in the pantry, refrigerator or icebox, and outside lockers. Menu planning is essential and can't be stressed enough.

How many meals will there be and for how many people? What access will there be to shops or markets? Do I know how to fish? (And, even if so, what is the likelihood of catching anything?) You will need to answer all of these questions before you get underway.

But even with the best-laid plans, there is always the unexpected. Weather is something that boaters are unable to control, and a well-stocked pantry can mean the difference between a wonderful meal in a bay tucked out of the storm or a less-than-stellar dinner made from odds and ends. And what about unexpected dinner guests? You should be prepared to host the couple you met while paddling to shore.

Having a good supply of different foods with a long shelf life is especially handy near the end of an extended cruise when provisions are at their lowest—or when you're looking for solitude and don't plan on making many stops to stock up.

In addition to the ingredients required to make specific recipes, you will also want to choose from the suggestions in the following pages to enhance your menu options and to have reserves. Be selective here. Keep in mind your personal preferences (and the dietary restrictions of you and your guests) and decide which ingredients you would use most often. If you would not use something more than once, leave it at home. The items listed below compliment the *Sea Salt* collection of recipes.

Aeriel's brightwork catches the morning light.

DRY GOODS

- pastas, quinoa, couscous, bulgur, rice noodles, lentils and quick-cooking rice
- shelled nuts and seeds, such as hazelnuts, walnuts, almonds, and sunflower and pumpkin seeds (toast a few in a piece of foil when you are cooking on the barbecue; they taste great sprinkled on a dessert or salad)
- dried fruit such as cranberries, apricots, cherries, blueberries, apples and raisins (to top cereal, oatmeal or dessert)
- rolled oats
- all-purpose flour
- sugar (granulated, unless a specific recipe requires otherwise)
- dehydrated mushrooms (for risottos, soups and pasta sauces)
- panko, Japanese-style bread crumbs (for a quick pasta topping or for breading fish)
- cured meat products such as dry salami that do not require refrigeration prior to opening

Tomato paste and sundried tomatoes add depth of flavour to a variety of dishes.

CANNED AND JARRED GOODS

- legumes (lentils, chickpeas)
- beans (black, white kidney, kidney)
- tomatoes (diced, paste, sauce, sun-dried)—a tube of tomato paste is handy to have on hand when only a small quantity is required
- pesto (a small jar will go a long way with pastas and pizzas on an extended cruise)
- pickled vegetables such as olives, artichokes, asparagus, green beans, red peppers and capers
- anchovy paste

BAKED GOODS

On an extended trip, sourcing fresh bread and cinnamon buns can become a ritual for boaters. One of the joys of boating is pulling into an unfamiliar anchorage, only to find a small bakery where fresh loaves have just been pulled out of the oven. That said, you must be prepared if your destination is far from such luxuries. Bring along a selection of baked goods with a longer shelf life, and ones that can be warmed quickly in the oven or on the barbecue.

- bread
- tortilla wraps
- flatbreads
- pitas
- English muffins
- baguettes, including varieties that can be finished off in the oven
- crackers
- cookies (to incorporate into quick desserts)

CONDIMENTS, ETC.

In addition to the homemade condiments listed in our condiments chapter (page 217), we suggest purchasing and bringing along the following items.

- jam
- liquid honey
- maple syrup
- natural peanut and/or almond butter
- Dijon mustard
- ketchup
- mayonnaise
- soy sauce or tamari
- hot sauce
- low-sodium chicken, beef and vegetable stock cubes

VINEGARS

- white wine vinegar
- red wine vinegar or balsamic vinegar

- pure olive oil or canola oil for cooking
- extra-virgin olive oil for salads and dips

DRIED HERBS AND SPICES

Use recently purchased herbs and spices packed in small zippered plastic bags. If you like to purchase larger quantities for your home kitchen, pack only what you think you'll need for the boating season; label and store the bags together in a plastic container with a lid that seals tightly. To retain their freshness, these items need to be kept dry. At the end of each boating season, take your spices and herbs home from the boat and use them up there. Do not leave them in the galley beyond one boating season. By the next spring it is unlikely that they will have any aroma when you open the bags.

Unless a recipe states otherwise, we use fine sea salt and freshly ground black pepper.

While many of our recipes call for fresh herbs, there may be times when they aren't available. In some cases, dried herbs may be substituted. When using dried herbs instead of fresh, the ratio is three parts fresh to one part dried. For example, 1 Tbsp (15 mL) fresh is equivalent to 1 tsp (5 mL) dry.

- fine sea salt
- coarse sea salt (rock or flakes)
- whole black peppercorns (to be ground as needed)
- oregano
- thyme
- basil
- dill
- rosemary
- cinnamon
- ground cumin

Dill, dry, in paste form or fresh, is a favourite herb in *Aeriel*'s galley.

- chili powder
- smoked paprika
- chipotle powder
- red pepper flakes
- cayenne
- bay leaves
- your favourite spice blends, such as steak spice

REFRIGERATOR AND ICEBOX

Dairy and Eggs

Choose milk, yogurt and other dairy products with the latest expiry date. Coffee cream that expires two days from now is not going to be pleasant in a week's time when you are anchored in your favourite bay, far from the nearest store and looking forward to your morning coffee. Store milk in a screw-top container with a spout. This helps to avoid spills in the refrigerator or icebox.

Before reaching into the dairy section, consider purchasing a milk substitute (soy, almond or rice)

These cured sausages from our local butcher shop do not require refrigeration.

or canned milk products (used for cooking), many of which only have to be refrigerated after they are opened. There are some excellent products available that have a much longer shelf life than dairy.

- butter (salted, unless a specific recipe requires otherwise)
- milk
- cream
- plain Greek-style yogurt (great with granola and in dips, dressings and sauces)
- selection of cheeses (for sandwiches or on the happy hour tray)—aged cheddar, a soft cheese such as brie or camembert, goat's cheese, parmesan
- mascarpone cheese (for quick desserts and savoury sauces)
- eggs or liquid eggs (compact containers store easily)

Meat

The best discovery that we have made—after several years of trial and error—is a vacuum packer. These handy gadgets ensure that food is airtight (prolonging its shelf life) and eliminates leaks in the refrigerator or icebox. In our Planning Ahead section (page 25), we address how the vacuum packer is a great tool to use for dishes prepared at home.

When packing meat for the boat, choose 6- to 8-oz (170- to 226-gr) portions that have little or no waste on them, such as boneless/skinless chicken breasts, strip loin steaks, pork tenderloin, lamb chops and sausages. You will save valuable space in the refrigerator or icebox.

Before heading out, vacuum pack your meat into meal-sized portions. Meat that will be grilled whole on the barbecue should be sealed into two-portion packages; meat that will be used in stir fries, pastas or threaded onto skewers for grilled kebabs should be cut into small cubes or strips. Freeze the meat at home. Not only will it last longer, but when frozen it acts as an ice pack. To thaw the meat safely, defrost it in the refrigerator.

If you're bringing along shaved deli meats for sandwiches or antipasto trays, bring only a small amount and eat it within a couple of days; keep in mind that turkey and chicken spoil much more quickly than cured meats such as ham and salami. For extended cruises, choose pre-packaged varieties, which have a longer shelf life.

- cured ham and salami (pre-sealed deli meats)
- dry, cured sausages (such as chorizo)
- fresh sausage (vacuum packed and frozen)
- uncooked chicken, beef, pork, lamb, duck and/or sausages (vacuum packed and frozen)

Seafood

Eating fresh fish is always optimal, however it's not always accessible on extended cruises (unless you're a skilled fisherman, of course). Rather than purchasing

Bill hauls up spot prawns in Drury Inlet, Broughton Archipelago. LORNA MALONE PHOTO

fresh seafood, only to freeze it as soon as you're home from the store, consider the impressive array of frozen-at-sea seafood available in your grocery store's freezer section. To know that you're getting a sustainable product, look for the "Ocean Wise Recommended" symbol.

Prior to cooking live shellfish, discard any that are chipped. Sharply tap any shellfish that are open. If they do not close, discard them. Clean shellfish under cold water, removing their beards (mussels). After cooking, discard any shellfish that are still closed.

- fresh fish and shellfish
- frozen-at-sea fish filets
- candied and smoked salmon
- locally processed canned seafood (tuna, salmon, smoked oysters and mussels)

Produce

As there is often limited space in the refrigerator or icebox, it's important to stock a basic selection of local, seasonal produce—organic, whenever possible—that is hardy enough to fare well in the outside lockers (where it's dark and dry). Instead of storing such foods in plastic bags, use well-ventilated mesh bags. The bags allow air to circulate, increasing the shelf life of your produce. Your potatoes are less likely to start sprouting.

Any vegetables that you plan to use for snacking with dip should be washed, peeled (if necessary), dried and cut, then stored in plastic food containers in the refrigerator or ice box.

The wonderful salad greens that we enjoy so much at home aren't practical for extended cruises as they spoil so quickly. Take along only what you'll need, to reduce unnecessary waste. Instead, experiment with cabbage, carrot, fennel and apple, along with your fresh herbs, to make vibrant, crunchy

Potatoes keep well in the outside lockers.

salads. Roasted vegetables, such as zucchini, tomatoes and bell peppers, are wonderful tossed with canned beans, couscous, quinoa or pasta for hearty salads. Cherry and grape tomatoes fare well on the counter.

To prevent spoilage in warm weather, nectarines, plums and fresh berries do need to be refrigerated and should be consumed during the earlier segment of your trip. Blueberries are an excellent choice as they last longer than other berries. Save hardy apples and pears for the latter part of your journey. Purchase your fruit firm and slightly under-ripe to extend its shelf life.

- root vegetables such as potatoes, squash, carrots, yams and beets

- tomatoes, bell peppers, zucchini and other favourite fresh vegetables
- onions, garlic and ginger root
- corn on the cob
- apples and pears
- lemons and limes
- soft fruits and fresh berries, for the first few days of the trip

Fresh Herbs and Aromatics

We suggest bringing along a selection of the following herbs, cut from your home garden or purchased at your local farmers' market. They should be rinsed, dried thoroughly and stored in dry paper towels in a plastic container in your refrigerator or icebox; some will last up to ten days this way. A few herbs in a root vegetable or pasta salad reduces the need for salad

PROVISIONING: LESSONS LEARNED

Ryan Malone (Lorna's son, and Alison and Hilary's brother) is part owner of Samara, a Vancouver-based sailboat. Reese Dawes, one of the owners, tells a cautionary tale about the first time he and third owner Peter Ramsden took Samara out on an extended cruise.

Prior to our Sunshine Coast cruise, Peter and I did the customary trading of emails regarding anchorage ideas and gear lists. In a blur of ignorant excitement, I volunteered to take care of provisioning the boat with food and drink; I was happy to help with something "easy." Our departure day arrived and, without making a list, I made my way to the grocery store. I filled my cart with four steaks, two

large packages of chicken, smokie sausages, black forest ham, two loaves of bread, a package of tortilla wraps, two dozen eggs, three heads of lettuce, eight tomatoes, two cucumbers, a bag of potatoes, several bell peppers, a bunch of bananas, eight ears of corn, a bag of oranges, a cantaloupe and a watermelon. As the cashier rang through my purchase at the till, I proudly told her that I was stocking up for a nine-day sailing trip.

When I arrived at *Samara*, I loaded the 15-plus bags of food into the tiny icebox, lockers, hatches, lazarette—and anywhere I could find a spare inch of space. At this point, I began to feel ill as I realized I had over-shopped and would have to ask the other two guys to split the very hefty grocery bill with me. Once we were underway, the other guys' jaws hit the cockpit as I admitted that I had gone overboard with my shopping.

The first sign of spoil came on day four, when the vegetables and fruit began getting soft and slimy. Embarrassed by my poor provisioning skills, I lightened the listing boat and cleared out the bulging food locker by secretly getting rid of the food. Overall, we threw out half of it. This was an expensive lesson to learn.

Since realizing that the BC coast is dotted with marinas and coastal towns, I have approached our cruising adventures very differently. I no longer provision with a navy fleet in mind. I now bring enough fresh food for two to four full days' worth of meals and supplement that with non-perishable snacks and starches from our well-stocked pantry. Thanks to a tip from Lorna, we now freeze our meat at home ahead of time. It lasts much longer that way and stretches out the life of the ice in the icebox.

greens, and they provide wonderful flavour and eye appeal, too.

On extended cruises, we stock a few herb pastes to use when our supply of fresh herbs is diminished. Packaged in tubes, they can be found in the cooler in your grocery store's produce section. These can add a burst of flavour to pastas, pizzas, soups, sauces and salad dressings.

- chives
- basil
- oregano
- thyme
- rosemary
- mint
- flat-leaf parsley
- cilantro

Things to consider when stocking your boat's refrigerator or icebox

Eliminate as much packaging as possible. If food is already sealed in plastic or vacuum packed, leave it in the packaging but eliminate all cardboard and other exterior wrapping. (Any cooking instructions on the exterior packaging can be written directly on the bag or on masking tape.)

Bring along small containers of any products that require refrigeration after opening.

Keep a supply of zippered freezer bags and plastic containers with tight-fitting lids on board. Foods such as cheese, deli meat and pre-cut vegetables should each be placed in their own containers to help keep the refrigerator or icebox organized.

Monitor the temperature in your refrigerator or icebox with a thermometer. It is generally recommended that the temperature be kept at 40F (4C).

BEVERAGES

There's something about the boating experience that makes you look forward to the next beverage. Perhaps it's the fact that as boaters we are constantly in tune with the weather. On a chilly, misty morning, nothing is better than the smell of fresh coffee wafting up from the galley; by that same token, a glass of chilled white wine or an icy-cold beer is almost as refreshing as a cooling dip in the ocean at the end of a warm summer's day.

Glass bottles occupy storage space and are at risk of breakage with all the movement on a boat, so we try to limit the amount of glass we bring aboard. As much as possible, we pack beverages that come in cans and Tetra Paks, which can later be flattened in preparation for recycling on land. If you're bringing wine, choose screw-top bottles or boxes that store easily once opened. When the refrigerator and outside lockers are near capacity, a diver's mesh bag hanging from the stern is a great way to chill canned beverages.

Planning Ahead

In order to help you plan your menu, some of the recipes are accompanied by the following icons:

MAKE AT HOME

The "Make at Home" symbol denotes dishes that are best baked or cooked at home and packed up for your journey. For most boaters, baking on board isn't a practical affair. While you may love to do so at home, keeping your galley oven heated for long periods of time uses up propane, and the required ingredients and supplies occupy storage space—not to mention the mess that often comes along with baking. If you're travelling in well-provisioned areas, part of the fun of venturing into a small community is seeking out a bakery with to-die-for artisanal loaves.

If baking on board is a top priority and your recipe doesn't take more than 30 minutes in the oven, consider measuring out your dry ingredients at home in order to cut down on preparation time.

VACUUM PACK AND FREEZE

When you are cruising in heavy weather, doing an overnight race with a full crew—or you're simply less inclined to cook on board and want something that can be made in advance—packing prepared meals is the best way to go. This is where the vacuum packer is worth its weight in gold. The vacuum-packing method keeps food airtight—preventing spoilage—and makes for quick clean-up. After preparing food at home, let it cool and package it into individual- or two-portion pouches and freeze them. In certain boating conditions, it's often the case that everyone aboard isn't able to eat at the same time. You don't want to open a package that serves eight and have most of the contents sit around on the stove until shift change.

When you are underway and want a hot, satisfying meal that is ready in minutes, simply drop the packages into a pot of water over a gas burner. Ideally you will have defrosted them in advance, but they can be cooked directly from frozen if time is an issue. Bring the water to a boil and then reduce the heat to a simmer. Cover until the pouches have heated through. Keep a close eye on the pot, as you do not want to overcook the contents.

Accompaniments such as potatoes, rice and couscous can be made fresh on board.

CHAPTER ONE

BREAKAWAY

Boaters often have a sense of anticipation as they push away from the dock on a Friday afternoon and certainly a feeling of relief that all the gear and groceries are safely stowed. There is always the joy that comes with the freedom of being at sea. Your first evening is cause for celebration—think coastal fresh with a glass of your favourite BC wine.

ISLAND SCALLOPS

Sweet, plump and firm, Qualicum Beach scallops are coveted by chefs and home cooks alike. The farmed Pacific scallops are the product of Island Scallops Ltd., launched in 1989 by owner Robert Saunders. The company operates a hatchery in Qualicum Bay and farms in the waters of Baynes Sound, Quadra Island and Georgia Strait. One of the largest scallops in the world, the Qualicum Beach scallop can reach up to 6 in (15 cm) in diameter and over 1 lb (454 gr) in weight. Qualicum Beach scallops can be purchased directly from the Island Scallops hatchery.

Seared Qualicum Beach Scallops with Sweetcorn-Basil Purée and Heirloom Tomato Salad

SERVES FOUR

On a warm summer evening, few things compare to a plate of fresh seafood and produce, prepared simply to allow the true flavours to shine through. This dish—perfect as a first course—showcases exquisite fresh scallops from Island Scallops, located north of Nanaimo in Qualicum Beach. Seared to perfection, they're served here with a creamy sweetcorn-basil purée and an heirloom tomato salad.

4 cobs corn, kernels removed from 3 cobs

3 Tbsp (45 mL) olive oil

1 small onion, diced

1 clove garlic, minced

½ cup (125 mL) whole milk

1 small handful basil leaves

Salt and pepper

1 cup (250 mL) coarsely chopped heirloom tomatoes

2 Tbsp (30 mL) coarsely chopped flat-leaf parsley

12 Qualicum Beach scallops

Over a gas burner or hot grill, char one cob of corn for approximately 10 minutes, rotating frequently. Remove kernels from the cob and set aside.

Heat 1 Tbsp (15 mL) olive oil in a small saucepan. Add onions and sweat until translucent. Add garlic and kernels from the three uncooked cobs. Cook until soft, approximately 4 minutes. Add milk and half the basil leaves and simmer for 2 minutes. Purée with an immersion blender until smooth. (A potato masher works just as well, producing a chunkier consistency.) Season to taste with salt and pepper and cover to keep warm.

Combine tomatoes, parsley, remaining basil leaves (torn), the charred corn kernels and 1 Tbsp (15 mL) olive oil in a small bowl.

Pat scallops dry with paper towels and season with salt and pepper. Add 1 Tbsp (15 mL) olive oil to a medium non-stick pan. Sear scallops until golden on both sides, approximately 2 minutes per side for large ones.

Spoon purée onto each plate. Top with three scallops and dress with heirloom tomato salad.

Cornmeal-Crusted Fanny Bay Oysters with Cucumber and Radish Salad

MAKES 12 OYSTERS

Dredged in a cornmeal crust and lightly fried, these oysters are served with a salad of cucumber, radishes and peppery watercress. We like to use fresh oysters from Mac's Oysters, located in Fanny Bay.

OYSTERS
¾ cup (180 mL) all-purpose flour

Pinch of cayenne

2 large eggs

1½ cups (350 mL) panko bread crumbs

½ cup (125 mL) cornmeal

Salt and pepper

12 fresh oysters, shucked

1 cup (250 mL) canola oil

CUCUMBER AND RADISH SALAD
1 small red onion, thinly sliced into half moons

1 small bunch radishes, cut into rounds

1 English cucumber, thinly sliced into rounds

1 small bunch watercress, stems discarded

¼ cup (60 mL) coarsely torn flat-leaf parsley

1 Tbsp (15 mL) olive oil

Salt and pepper

TO SERVE
¾ cup (180 mL) Lemon and Dill Yogurt (page 228)

OYSTERS Mix flour and cayenne together in a small bowl. In a second bowl, whisk eggs. In a third bowl, combine panko and cornmeal. Season ingredients in all three bowls with salt and pepper.

Pat oysters dry with paper towels. Lightly dredge them in flour, dip them in beaten eggs and then coat in the panko mixture, pressing lightly to help the crumbs adhere. Set aside.

In a non-stick sauté pan, heat canola oil over high heat until a pinch of flour sizzles when added. Working in small batches to ensure that the oil remains hot, fry oysters, turning once, until the coating is crisp and golden, 2 to 3 minutes per side. Drain on paper towels.

CUCUMBER AND RADISH SALAD In a medium bowl, mix red onions, radishes, cucumbers, watercress and parsley. Dress with olive oil and season to taste with salt and pepper.

TO SERVE Arrange oysters on a platter and spoon cucumber salad on the side. Serve with Lemon and Dill Yogurt.

MAC'S OYSTERS LTD.

A tiny community located on the east coast of Vancouver Island, Fanny Bay is known for its sweet, plump oysters. The bivalve molluscs first came to the area in 1947 when Joseph McLellan imported 300 lbs (136 kg) of oyster seed from Japan. The pioneering Scotsman— who had settled in the community in the early twentieth century—seeded the beaches of Baynes Sound in hopes of farming an oyster far superior than the indigenous Olympia variety. Today, McLellan's legacy is carried on by his children and grandchildren, who operate Mac's Oysters Ltd. and sell beach-harvest, beach-hardened and deep-water varieties, along with live clams.

A full moon rises over Cortes Island.
Photo taken from Shark Spit, Marina Island.
JULIE BEAUREGARD-STEWART PHOTO

Parmesan Polenta with Mushroom Ragout

SERVES FOUR

When you want to serve an elegant, vegetarian main dish, look no further than this recipe for rich mushroom ragout piled atop a bed of creamy parmesan polenta.

PARMESAN POLENTA

4 cups (1 L) vegetable stock

1 tsp (5 mL) salt

1 cup (250 mL) cornmeal

⅓ cup (80 mL) whipping cream

2 Tbsp (30 mL) butter

¼ cup (60 mL) grated parmesan cheese, plus more for garnish

Salt and pepper

MUSHROOM RAGOUT

2 Tbsp (30 mL) butter

1 Tbsp (15 mL) olive oil

1 shallot, sliced

2 cloves garlic, minced

1 sprig thyme, leaves removed

4 cups (1 L) coarsely chopped mixed mushrooms (we use oyster, chanterelle and crimini)

¼ cup (60 mL) red wine

⅓ cup (80 mL) whipping cream

¼ cup (60 mL) coarsely chopped flat-leaf parsley

Salt and pepper

PARMESAN POLENTA Bring vegetable stock and salt to a boil in a large saucepan. Whisk in cornmeal and reduce heat to low. Simmer for 10 to 15 minutes, stirring frequently, until cornmeal has softened. Stir in cream, butter and parmesan cheese. Season to taste with salt and pepper.

MUSHROOM RAGOUT Over medium-high heat, combine butter and olive oil in a sauté pan. Add shallots and cook until translucent, approximately 3 minutes. Add garlic and thyme and cook until fragrant, approximately 30 seconds. Add mushrooms and sauté until soft and lightly browned, approximately 8 minutes.

Add red wine to mushrooms and cook until liquid has reduced by half, approximately 4 minutes. Add cream and parsley and warm through. Season to taste with salt and pepper.

Serve ragout over polenta on individual plates. Garnish servings with additional parmesan cheese.

SEA CIDER FARM & CIDERHOUSE

Inheriting an apple orchard on Shuswap Lake as a teenager served as Kristen Jordan's first introduction to the craft of cider-making. Decades later, with a desire to pursue her hobby full time, Jordan purchased a sheep farm on the east coast of Saanich Peninsula and planted 1,000 apple trees. Assisted by her brother, mother and uncles, she now operates Sea Cider Farm & Ciderhouse, an award-winning artisan cidery producing eight heritage styles of small-batch, hard apple cider. In addition to the 60 varieties of certified organic apples—primarily French and British cider varieties—that are grown on site, Sea Cider also sources apples from local growers. After apples are harvested between August and October, they are hand-pressed and fermented with champagne yeasts using traditional methods. Sea Cider offers tastings in the ciderhouse, which boasts views of Cordova Strait and James Island beyond. Sea Cider Farm & Ciderhouse's products are sold at Liquor Plus stores in Victoria, Saanich, Cobble Hill and Duncan, as well as other private liquor stores and wine shops.

Grilled Flatbreads

SERVES ONE OR MORE

In the summer, when you're more inclined to cook on the barbecue and less so to turn on your oven, grill a few flatbread pizzas to serve with drinks, such as chilled bottles of cider from Sea Cider Farm & Ciderhouse. Simple combinations of good-quality ingredients, say three or four per pizza, are all you need. Two of our favourite combinations are radicchio, goat's brie and fig jam, and prosciutto, parmesan and arugula. Keep a package of store-bought flatbreads on hand so that you're free to experiment whenever the mood strikes. We're not fussed with exact measurements when preparing casual food like this.

Flatbreads (1 per person for a meal, less as an appetizer)

Extra-virgin olive oil

Salt and pepper

RADICCHIO, GOAT'S BRIE AND FIG JAM

Head(s) radicchio, sliced in half lengthwise

Fig jam

Goat's brie

Microgreens (optional)

PROSCIUTTO, PARMESAN AND ARUGULA

Mozzarella cheese, grated

Parmesan cheese, sliced into shards

Prosciutto

Arugula

RADICCHIO, GOAT'S BRIE AND FIG JAM

Preheat barbecue to medium. Brush radicchio with olive oil and season with salt and pepper. Grill until it begins to wilt, approximately 3 minutes on each side. Remove outer layer and chop roughly.

Grill flatbread on both sides, approximately 2 minutes per side.

Top flatbread with a thin layer of fig jam and pieces of goat's brie. Close the barbecue and grill until cheese has melted, approximately 3 minutes. Remove the pizza from the barbecue and top with radicchio and microgreens, if using.

PROSCIUTTO, PARMESAN AND ARUGULA

Preheat barbecue to medium. Grill flatbread on both sides, approximately 2 minutes per side.

Top flatbread with mozzarella cheese and parmesan cheese and grill with the barbecue closed until the mozzarella has melted, approximately 3 minutes. Remove the pizza from the barbecue and top with slices of prosciutto and arugula.

Smoked Black Cod and Cheddar Chowder

SERVES FOUR

Every galley cook should have a seafood chowder in his or her repertoire. It's hot, satisfying and can be made with any fresh, readily available fish or shellfish. This version showcases black cod (also known as sablefish), an oily, firm-textured fish that comes into its own when smoked. Smoked paprika imparts further depth, while aged cheddar cheese adds richness. In a downpour, steaming bowls of this chowder are always appreciated.

2 medium potatoes, peeled and diced

¼ cup (60 mL) unsalted butter

¼ cup (60 mL) finely chopped onion

¼ cup (60 mL) finely chopped celery

¼ cup (60 mL) all-purpose flour

1 tsp (5 mL) smoked paprika

2 × 10 fl oz (284 mL) cans clam nectar

1 Tbsp (15 mL) tomato paste

¼ cup (60 mL) finely chopped red (or orange) bell peppers

1½ cups (350 mL) whole milk

Salt and pepper

1 lb (454 gr) boneless/skinless smoked black cod, cut into 1-in (2.5-cm) pieces

¾ cup (180 mL) fresh or canned kernel corn

½ cup (125 mL) grated aged cheddar cheese

2 tsp (10 mL) minced chives

2 tsp (10 mL) minced flat-leaf parsley

Boil potatoes in a small saucepan of salted water until cooked but still firm, approximately 6 minutes. Drain and set aside.

Melt butter in a medium saucepan over medium heat. Add onions and celery and cook until softened, about 3 minutes. Stir in flour and paprika until thoroughly incorporated, then whisk in clam nectar and tomato paste. Bring broth to a boil, then turn down the heat and simmer. Add bell peppers. Cook, stirring frequently, for 10 minutes. Add milk and heat through.

Season to taste with salt and pepper, then add cod, corn and pre-cooked potatoes. Simmer for 5 minutes or until cod is just cooked through. Add cheese, chives and parsley and stir until cheese is melted. Serve immediately.

Salt Spring Island Mussels with Fennel and Ale

MAKES TWO LARGE SERVINGS (OR FOUR STARTER-SIZED SERVINGS)

Sweet and succulent, Salt Spring Island mussels are adored by locals and sought out by visitors. In this dish, fennel punctuates a rich broth made with local ale. (As the recipe only calls for half a bottle, we encourage you to sip the other half while you cook.) Serve heaping bowls of mussels alongside crusty baguettes for soaking up the flavourful broth.

2 lbs (908 gr) Salt Spring Island mussels

1 Tbsp (15 mL) olive oil

1 large shallot, minced

2 cloves garlic, minced

1 medium fennel bulb, cut in half lengthwise and sliced very thinly

1 heaping tsp (5–7 mL) Dijon mustard

1 × 12 fl oz (341 mL) bottle ale

1 Tbsp (15 mL) butter

¼ cup (60 mL) whipping cream

Salt and pepper

3 Tbsp (45 mL) coarsely chopped flat-leaf parsley

Fennel fronds from 1 bulb, coarsely chopped

Discard any mussels that are chipped. Sharply tap any mussels that are open. If they do not close, discard them. Clean the mussels under cold water, removing their beards.

Warm olive oil in a large pot over medium heat. Add shallots and garlic and sweat until soft. Add fennel and cook until tender, approximately 5 minutes. Stir in mustard and ale. Add mussels. Cover and cook over medium heat for 6 minutes or until mussels have opened. Add the butter and cream and warm through. Season to taste with salt and pepper. Add parsley and fennel fronds and stir through. Remove from heat and discard any mussels that are still closed. Serve immediately.

ISLAND SEA FARMS

In the organic farming community, the Gulf Islands are known for their dedication to sustainable food production. This rings true beyond the islands' gardens and fields to the waters that surround them. Here, mussels grow year round, thanks to the Japanese kuroshio current that brings nutrient-rich waters to the south coast. Since 1996, Island Sea Farms has been growing the Mediterranean (*Mytilus galloprovincialis*) and Atlantic Blue (*Mytilus edulis*) varieties—along with several hybrids—heralded for being characteristically sweet and plump. Founder and president Paul Simpson and his longstanding crew of fellow Gulf Islanders operate their hatchery and nursery on Salt Spring Island and conduct much of their grow-out on Cortes Island. The team farms their mussels naturally using deep-water rope-grown methods and is a leader in the field of high-tech seed production. Salt Spring Island mussels are available at Thrifty Foods and Country Grocer.

Pacific Cioppino

SERVES FOUR

Our West Coast version of the classic Italian cioppino, this showstopper seafood dish is perfect for a special al fresco dinner for four. While we like to use a combination of salmon, firm white fish (halibut, cod or red snapper) and shellfish (scallops, spot prawns and clams or mussels), it's really a matter of both personal preference and what is available fresh. Serve with a green salad and a crusty loaf of artisanal bread to mop up the saffron-infused tomato broth.

1 lb (454 gr) clams and/or mussels, cleaned and de-bearded

2 Tbsp (30 mL) olive oil

½ small onion, diced

2 small carrots, diced

2 celery stalks, diced

2 cloves garlic, minced

½ tsp (2.5 mL) sweet paprika

Pinch of saffron

½ tsp (2.5 mL) fennel seeds, crushed

½ tsp (2.5 mL) coriander seeds

1 cup (250 mL) white wine

1 × 28 fl oz (796 mL) can diced tomatoes

2 × 10 fl oz (284 mL) cans clam nectar

Salt and pepper

1 lb (454 gr) fish (combination of salmon and whitefish such as halibut, cod or red snapper)

1 lb (454 gr) scallops and/or spot prawns

Parsley for garnish

Discard any clams or mussels that are chipped, and any clams that are open, prior to cooking. Sharply tap any mussels that are open. If they do not close, discard them.

Pour olive oil into a stockpot and warm over medium heat. Add onions, carrots, celery and garlic. Cook until softened, approximately 5 minutes. Add paprika, saffron, fennel seeds and coriander seeds and toast until fragrant. Add white wine and simmer for 5 minutes. Add tomatoes and clam nectar. Bring to a boil, then lower the heat and let simmer for 15 minutes.

Season broth to taste with salt and pepper. Add all seafood, place lid on pot and heat until fish is cooked and clams and mussels are open, approximately 5 minutes. Remove from heat and discard any shellfish that are still closed.

Ladle broth and seafood into serving bowls. Garnish with parsley.

Baked Halibut with Tomato Salsa

SERVES FOUR

In this recipe, the halibut is marinated then cooked on the barbecue in a foil packet, yielding an incredibly moist, tender texture. Once you have tried this recipe, you may not want to cook halibut any other way. Served over Puy lentils and topped with tomato salsa, this dish is not only delicious but also has great eye appeal. Rice, couscous and quinoa work equally well in place of the lentils.

4 pieces halibut, each 6 oz (170 gr), even thickness with skin removed

1 cup (250 mL) uncooked Puy lentils

1 small handful cilantro leaves, to garnish

MARINADE

½ cup (125 mL) white wine

¼ cup (60 mL) minced white onion

2 Tbsp (30 mL) minced garlic

2 Tbsp (30 mL) olive oil

SALSA

1 lb (454 gr) heirloom tomatoes, of different types, coarsely chopped

¼ cup (60 mL) roughly chopped cilantro

Juice of 1 lime

Pinch of red pepper flakes

Pinch of salt

2 Tbsp (30 mL) extra-virgin olive oil

MARINADE ⟿ Combine the marinade ingredients in an airtight container. Add halibut and turn to coat. Marinate filets in the refrigerator or ice-box for one hour, turning once.

SALSA ⟿ Combine all salsa ingredients in a medium bowl and set aside.

TO ASSEMBLE ⟿ In a medium saucepan, combine lentils with three cups water. Bring to a boil, then reduce heat and simmer uncovered until lentils are cooked through but al dente, approximately 20 minutes.

Preheat barbecue to medium-high. Remove halibut from marinade and place filets in well-sealed, individual foil packets, leaving some space at the top for steam. Place packets on barbecue and cook for 12 minutes.

Lay halibut over a bed of lentils on each plate and top with salsa and torn cilantro leaves. ⤶

Seared Chèvre with Seasonal Greens and Heirloom Tomatoes

SERVES FOUR

In this dish, seasonal greens and heirloom tomatoes are made into a substantial first course with the addition of wonderful seared chèvre. Rounds of goat's cheese are breaded and toasted in a pan, yielding a beautifully creamy centre. Serve with fresh bread, purchased at your favourite bakery before leaving port.

¼ cup (60 mL) all-purpose flour

1 egg, beaten

½ cup (125 mL) panko bread crumbs

Salt and pepper

8 oz (226 gr) goat's cheese, cut into ½-in (1.3-cm) rounds

¼ cup (60 mL) plus 1 Tbsp (15 mL) olive oil

4 heirloom tomatoes, sliced into rounds

2 tsp (10 mL) balsamic vinegar

Mixed seasonal greens

1 handful mixed fresh herbs (we use flat-leaf parsley, mint and basil)

Set up a breading station by placing flour, egg and panko into three separate bowls. Season each with salt and pepper. Coat goat's cheese rounds in flour, then dip in egg. Dredge in panko.

Heat 2 Tbsp (30 mL) olive oil in a medium non-stick pan over medium heat. Fry goat's cheese rounds until golden, approximately 3 minutes per side.

Drizzle tomatoes with 2 Tbsp (30 mL) olive oil and balsamic vinegar. Toss mixed greens with herbs and the remaining 1 Tbsp (15 mL) olive oil. Season to taste with salt and pepper.

Arrange tomatoes on a platter and top with herb salad. Top with seared chèvre.

HILARY'S CHEESE

Based in the idyllic seaside hamlet of Cowichan Bay, Hilary's Cheese was established in 2001 by husband and wife team Hilary and Patty Abbott. Guided by artisan techniques, the couple uses goat's and cow's milk from local farmers to produce small, handmade batches of white bloom, washed rind, fresh and blue cheeses. After anchoring your boat in the bay, wander up to the shop and sit down for lunch; the on-site café serves artisanal sandwiches using bread from neighbour True Grain Bread (page 78). Hilary's Cheese operates a location in Victoria, as well.

Pear and Blackberry Galette

SERVES SIX

French in origin, a galette is a rustic, free-form pie made with a rich, flaky crust and piled high with a sweet or savoury filling. As it doesn't have to fit into a pie plate, it is much easier to assemble than a traditional pie. While the pastry can be made easily in a food processor, packaged, refrigerated pie dough is an excellent shortcut. We love to make sweet galettes year-round, highlighting fresh seasonal fruit. This version showcases pears and blackberries, but the combinations are endless.

PASTRY
1½ cups (350 mL) all-purpose flour
½ tsp (2.5 mL) salt
½ cup (125 mL) chilled, unsalted butter, cut into small pieces
4–6 Tbsp (60–90 mL) ice water

FILLING
1 Tbsp (15 mL) cornstarch
½ cup (125 mL) granulated sugar
2 large ripe pears, peeled, cored and cubed
2 cups (475 mL) blackberries
1 Tbsp (15 mL) unsalted butter, cut into small cubes
1 egg, beaten
Fine berry sugar

PASTRY In a food processor, mix flour and salt. Add butter and pulse until mixture resembles coarse meal. Add ice water all at once, and pulse until mixture starts to hold together; stop before it forms a ball. Shape dough into a disc and refrigerate for 30 minutes before using.

Preheat oven to 400F (205C). Roll out pastry on a lightly floured surface to a circle 14-in (36-cm) in diameter. Transfer to a parchment paper–lined baking sheet.

FILLING In a large bowl, combine cornstarch and granulated sugar. Add pears and blackberries. Mix gently to avoid crushing the berries. Place fruit mixture into the middle of the pastry, leaving a 3-in (7.6-cm) border around the edge. Dot with cubes of butter. Lift the edges of the pastry up onto the filling, leaving some space in the middle where the fruit is exposed.

Brush the pastry with egg and sprinkle with berry sugar. Bake for 45 minutes or until bubbly and golden. While cooking, pastry may be tented with foil to prevent it from becoming too brown.

Remove from oven and slide parchment paper and galette onto a cooling rack. Cool completely before storing. For transportation to the boat, carry the galette in a large round container with a tight-fitting lid.

Sea Salt and Caramel Brownies

MAKES 16 BROWNIES

These moist, fudgy brownies will vanish almost instantly when presented to your guests. The sweet caramel is beautifully offset by a subtle sprinkling of rock salt. We love to use rock salt from the Vancouver Island Salt Co., based in Cobble Hill.

BROWNIES
¾ cup (180 mL) unsalted butter

2 oz (56 gr) unsweetened chocolate, finely chopped

2 cups (475 mL) granulated sugar

3 large eggs

1½ tsp (7.5 mL) vanilla extract

1 cup (250 mL) all-purpose flour

¼ cup (60 mL) plus 2 Tbsp (30 mL) unsweetened cocoa

CARAMEL
¾ cup (180 mL) granulated sugar

⅓ cup (80 mL) light corn syrup

3 Tbsp (45 mL) water

Pinch of salt

⅓ cup (80 mL) whipping cream

1 tsp (5 mL) vanilla extract

GARNISH
Rock salt

BROWNIES Preheat oven to 350F (175C). Line a 9-in (23-cm) square metal cake pan with parchment paper. Spray paper lightly with cooking oil. Set aside.

In a large saucepan, melt butter with chocolate over low heat, stirring occasionally. Remove from heat and cool to room temperature.

Whisk together sugar, eggs and vanilla in a large bowl. Slowly add chocolate mixture, stirring until thoroughly incorporated. Sift flour and cocoa together and fold into batter until just combined. Pour batter into the prepared pan and smooth the surface.

Bake brownies in the middle of the oven for approximately 35 minutes, until the edges are set and a toothpick inserted into the centre comes out clean. Cool at room temperature in the pan for 1 hour.

CARAMEL Bring sugar, corn syrup, water and salt to a boil in a heavy saucepan over medium heat, stirring until the sugar is dissolved. Boil, without stirring, until mixture turns a golden caramel colour, approximately 10 minutes. Remove from heat and stir in cream and vanilla.

TO ASSEMBLE Pour caramel over the brownies, spreading evenly. Cool completely in the pan in the refrigerator.

Once brownies are cooled, scatter rock salt over top. Gripping the edges of the parchment paper, lift brownies from the pan. Remove paper. Cut brownies into 16 squares. Store in the refrigerator in an airtight container and serve at room temperature.

VANCOUVER ISLAND SALT CO.

Over a decade working as a chef in Canada, Australia and New Zealand exposed Andrew Shepherd to a world of fine foods. In 2010, yearning to spend more time at home with his children, the Cobble Hill resident shifted his professional focus and established the Vancouver Island Salt Co., the first commercial sea salt harvestry in Canada. Shepherd forages for salt in the tidal waters off Cherry Point and transforms his bounty into the company's Infused Sea Salts (roasted garlic, balsamic, blue cheese, Spanish paprika, mustard, banana peppers, bacon and jerk) and Smoked Canadian Rock Salts (maple, cherry and alder), which enhance the flavour of foods both savoury and sweet. Vancouver Island Salt Co. products are available at Country Grocer and Fairway Markets.

CHAPTER TWO

BRUNCH

At home, brunch is often reserved for leisurely mornings, but when you are on the boat it can be enjoyed any day of the week. Whether you fancy something sweet or savoury, you'll find it among these dishes, any of which would be perfect after an early paddle in the kayak or before you settle into that great book with your second cup of coffee.

Mushrooms on Toast with Poached Eggs and Seasonal Greens

SERVES TWO

Beautifully creamy and rich in flavour, these mushrooms are delicious on thick slices of toasted country bread. Poached eggs and seasonal greens round out the dish. Don't let the list of ingredients deter you. This recipe comes together quite quickly and is well worth the effort.

2 Tbsp (30 mL) butter

2 Tbsp (30 mL) canola oil

4 cups (1 L) mixed mushrooms (such as brown, crimini, oyster), coarsely chopped

1 shallot, minced

1 clove garlic, minced

⅓ cup (80 mL) beef stock

¼ cup (60 mL) whipping cream

2 Tbsp (30 mL) Marsala (optional)

Salt and pepper

1 Tbsp (15 mL) finely chopped flat-leaf parsley

1 Tbsp (15 mL) white vinegar

2 eggs

2 thick slices country bread

2 small handfuls mixed, seasonal baby greens

2 tsp (10 mL) olive oil

In a deep-sided sauté pan over medium-high heat, combine butter and canola oil. Sauté mushrooms with shallots and garlic until mushrooms are cooked through. Add beef stock, whipping cream and Marsala, if using, and continue cooking until the sauce has reduced by half, approximately 5 minutes. Remove from heat. Season to taste with salt and pepper and stir in parsley.

Bring a small saucepan of water just to a boil, then reduce heat to medium-low. Add vinegar and crack the eggs into the water. Poach until the yolks are cooked to the desired degree, 3 to 5 minutes. Remove eggs with a slotted spoon, dabbing the undersides with a clean dishtowel to absorb excess water.

While the eggs are poaching, toast bread and toss greens with olive oil in a small bowl.

Set one slice of toast on each plate. Top each with mushrooms, an egg and greens. Serve immediately.

Sablefish Frittata with Asparagus, Red Peppers and Goat's Cheese

SERVES FOUR

Easily prepared in one pan, a frittata is the perfect egg dish to serve to a group. Sablefish, a beautiful oily fish caught off the coast of BC, tastes terrific with asparagus, red peppers and goat's cheese. While frittatas are usually finished in the oven, we've cut down on cooking time by covering the pan and cooking it entirely on the stove. We love to serve this dish with our Habanero and Red Pepper Jelly (page 224).

1 Tbsp (15 mL) olive oil

1 sablefish filet, 8–12 oz (225–338 gr), pin bones removed

8 eggs

2 Tbsp (30 mL) chopped fresh chives, plus more for garnish

Salt and pepper

1 small shallot, finely diced

¼ cup (60 mL) finely diced red peppers

3 asparagus spears, cut diagonally into 2-in (5-cm) pieces

4 oz (112 gr) goat's cheese

In a stainless steel pan with a lid, warm olive oil over medium-high heat. Place sablefish in the pan, skin side down, and cook for 3 minutes. Flip fish and pan-fry until just cooked through. Remove the skin from the filet and set fish aside.

In a small bowl, whisk eggs with chopped chives, a pinch of salt and freshly ground black pepper.

In the same pan used for the fish, over medium heat, partially cook shallots, red peppers and asparagus, about 6 minutes. Spread vegetables out evenly in the pan. Reduce heat to low and pour in egg mixture. Do not stir. Cook until frittata has partially set, about 5 minutes. Flake sablefish and crumble goat's cheese over the frittata. Cover with a lid and let cook for 2 to 3 minutes more. Remove from heat.

Cut frittata into wedges and serve right out of the pan. Garnish with chopped fresh chives.

Eggs Baked in Spicy Tomatoes

SERVES TWO

If you wake up to a sunny day, go for a morning dip to build up your appetite before tucking into this hearty breakfast. This is our take on shakshuka, a North African dish of eggs poached in an aromatic tomato sauce. Serve with plenty of toasted artisanal bread—it will taste delicious dipped in the runny egg yolks.

¼ tsp (1 mL) cumin seeds

2 Tbsp (30 mL) olive oil

1 small onion, thinly sliced

2 cloves garlic, finely minced

2 yellow peppers, thinly sliced

½ tsp (2.5 mL) granulated sugar

1½ cups (350 mL) canned tomato purée

¼ cup (60 mL) water

Pinch of saffron

Pinch of cayenne

1 bay leaf

3 sprigs thyme, leaves removed

1 Tbsp (15 mL) roughly chopped parsley

2 Tbsp (30 mL) roughly chopped cilantro

Salt and pepper

4 eggs

4 slices bread

¼ cup (60 mL) crumbled feta cheese

Heat a sauté pan over medium heat. Add cumin seeds and toast until fragrant, approximately 30 seconds. Add olive oil, onions, garlic and peppers and sauté until softened, approximately 5 minutes. Add sugar, tomato purée, water, saffron, cayenne, bay leaf, thyme, parsley and 1 Tbsp (15 mL) cilantro. Season to taste with salt and pepper. Simmer for 5 minutes.

Break eggs onto the top of the tomato mixture. Reduce heat to low and simmer, covered, until the eggs are just set, approximately 10 minutes. When the eggs are just about done, toast the bread.

Sprinkle eggs and tomatoes with crumbled feta cheese and remaining cilantro. Serve with toasted bread.

Lox with Fried Eggs and Caper and Herb Béarnaise

SERVES FOUR

Paper-thin slices of lox are a wonderful way to incorporate salmon into your brunch menu. In this twist on eggs Benedict, we've set lox and a fried egg atop a toasted bagel and draped it all with caper and herb Béarnaise.

CAPER AND HERB BÉARNAISE

4 egg yolks

2 tsp (10 mL) white wine vinegar

½ cup (125 mL) unsalted butter, cubed

2 tsp (10 mL) capers, chopped

¼ cup (60 mL) minced herbs
(we use parsley, tarragon and dill)

Salt and pepper

TO ASSEMBLE

1 tsp (5 mL) butter

1 tsp (5 mL) olive oil

4 eggs

2 whole-grain bagels (or bread
of your choice)

12–16 slices lox

CAPER AND HERB BÉARNAISE ⟿ Set a stainless-steel mixing bowl over a saucepan of simmering water. Put egg yolks in the bowl. Whisking constantly, add white wine vinegar and then butter, melting one cube at a time. Whisk until thickened and pale in colour. Add capers and herbs and season to taste with salt and pepper.

TO ASSEMBLE ⟿ In a large sauté pan over medium-high heat, combine butter and olive oil. Crack eggs into the pan and fry until whites are firm and yolks are just set.

Split and toast bagels. Set one half of a bagel on each plate and top with lox. Top with eggs and caper and herb Béarnaise. ⟿

TOP LEFT: Downwind in Johnstone Strait.
MIKE PEPLER PHOTO

TOP RIGHT: A charming classic sailing vessel sits
at anchor in Clam Bay. LORNA MALONE PHOTO

BOTTOM: A grizzly bear is observed from
a safe distance in Orford Bay, Bute Inlet.
JULIE BEAUREGARD–STEWART PHOTO

Black Bean Breakfast Wrap

SERVES FOUR

Bursting with bright, fresh flavours, this wrap is our take on huevos rancheros, a beloved Mexican breakfast dish. Try it on a lazy morning when you're looking for something different to start the day. You can cut down on your preparation time by making the hot pickle and spicy black beans at home (keep both mixtures refrigerated). Simply reheat the black beans at serving time.

HOT PICKLE

¼ cup (60 mL) apple cider vinegar

1 tsp (5 mL) granulated sugar

½ tsp (2.5 mL) salt

½ red onion, thinly sliced

½ jalapeno pepper, thinly sliced

8 radishes, thinly sliced

SPICY BLACK BEANS

1 Tbsp (15 mL) olive oil

½ small onion, sliced

1 clove garlic, minced

¾ tsp (3.5 mL) ground cumin

¾ tsp (3.5 mL) chili powder

1 × 14 fl oz (398 mL) can black beans, drained but not rinsed

Pepper

TO ASSEMBLE

4 large tortilla wraps

4 eggs

1 Tbsp (15 mL) butter

1 avocado, cut into slices

¼ cup (60 mL) roughly chopped cilantro

1 × 3.5 oz (100 gr) package sunflower sprouts

⅓ cup (80 mL) crumbled queso fresco (or feta cheese)

HOT PICKLE ⟿ Whisk the first three ingredients in a small bowl with 1 cup (250 mL) water. Stir until sugar and salt dissolve. Add onions, jalapeno peppers and radishes. Refrigerate in an airtight container. Before serving, allow to sit at room temperature for a minimum of 30 minutes.

SPICY BLACK BEANS ⟿ Heat olive oil over medium-high heat in a non-stick sauté pan. Add onions and cook until softened, about 3 minutes. Add garlic, cumin and chili powder and cook for 30 seconds. Add beans and 2 Tbsp (30 mL) water. Cook until warmed through. Season to taste with pepper. (There is no need to add additional salt as the bean liquid is salty enough.)

TO ASSEMBLE ⟿ Warm tortillas in the oven or in a pan on the stove. Meanwhile, reheat spicy black beans (if prepared ahead of time) in a small pot and fry eggs in butter in a sauté pan over medium-high heat until whites are firm and yolks are set but still runny, about 4 minutes. Top each tortilla with spicy black beans, a fried egg, hot pickle, avocado, cilantro, sunflower sprouts and queso fresco. Wrap tightly. ⤺

Candied Salmon and Corn Fritters

MAKES FOUR TO SIX FRITTERS

A delicious addition to our morning menu, these simple corn fritters are made with sweet fresh corn and beautiful candied salmon. We use the candied salmon nuggets from Hardy Buoys, located in the north island town of Port Hardy. To simplify your on-board preparation, we suggest measuring out the first five dry ingredients at home and packing the mixture along in a zippered plastic bag.

⅓ cup (80 mL) cornmeal

⅓ cup (80 mL) all-purpose flour

½ tsp (2.5 mL) baking soda

Salt and pepper

1 egg

⅓ cup (80 mL) whole milk

¼ cup (60 mL) cream cheese, softened

Kernels from 1 cooked cob of corn, approximately ¾ cup (180 mL)

3 Tbsp (45 mL) minced chives

⅓ cup (80 mL) crumbled candied salmon

2 tsp (10 mL) canola oil

Habanero and Red Pepper Jelly (page 224)

Sour cream

In a bowl, combine cornmeal, flour and baking soda. Add a pinch each of salt and pepper. In a separate bowl, whisk together the egg, milk and cream cheese. Finely chop half the corn kernels. Add chopped and whole kernels to the wet mixture and combine well. Stir the dry mixture into the wet mixture. Fold in chives and salmon.

Over medium-high heat, heat a medium non-stick pan and coat with canola oil. For each fritter, drop about ¼ cup (60 mL) of the mixture into the pan. Cook the fritters until golden brown, approximately 3 minutes a side. Drain on paper towels.

Serve with Habanero and Red Pepper Jelly and sour cream. For a sweeter version, omit the chives and serve with maple syrup.

HARDY BUOYS
SMOKED FISH INC.

What began as a love of fishing has grown into a full-time fish-processing business for Bruce Dirom. In 1994, he and his wife, Carol, founded Hardy Buoys in Port Hardy, a small fishing town on the northeastern tip of Vancouver Island. Using pure alder chips, the Diroms and their team transform locally caught salmon into a variety of hot- and cold-smoked products, including candied salmon and smoked salmon, that are available in different flavours. While Hardy Buoys is now one of Port Hardy's largest employers, the Diroms plan to keep their business family-run by having their oldest son, Dylan—who started working with them at age 11, washing buckets—continue to grow the company. Boaters and fishermen who make big catches in local waters may arrange to have Hardy Buoys pick up and process their bounty. Hardy Buoys' smoked fish products are available at Thrifty Foods, Save-On Foods, Walmart, Safeway and Sobey's.

Chorizo and Red Pepper Hash with Poached Eggs

SERVES TWO

This breakfast hash of crispy potatoes, spicy chorizo sausage, sweet red peppers and perfectly poached eggs is a great dish to serve to friends when it's your turn to host brunch. As the potatoes and dried chorizo have a long shelf life, it is also a good choice for the end of your journey.

2 yellow-skinned potatoes, peeled and diced in small pieces

2 Tbsp (30 mL) canola oil

1 Tbsp (15 mL) butter

½ onion, chopped

½ red pepper, chopped (or ⅓ cup/80 mL chopped roasted red peppers)

½ tsp (2.5 mL) dried oregano

1 link dried chorizo sausage, casing removed and sliced into thin rounds

1 Tbsp (15 mL) white vinegar

4 eggs

¼ cup (60 mL) grated parmesan cheese

2 tsp (10 mL) chopped herbs (optional)

Put potatoes in a large, deep-sided sauté pan and cover with water. Bring to a boil and cook over medium heat until the potatoes are tender when pierced with the tip of a knife but not cooked through, approximately 6 minutes. Drain. Add canola oil and butter to the pan and fry potatoes until brown and crispy, approximately 15 minutes.

When the potatoes are about halfway done, move them to one side of pan and add onions, peppers and oregano to other side. Cook this mixture until soft, but do not mix with the potatoes. When potatoes and vegetables are nearly done, create a space in the middle of the pan for the chorizo slices. Cook for 3 more minutes or until chorizo is heated through. Remove from heat and cover to keep warm.

Bring a small saucepan of water just to a boil, then reduce heat to medium-low and simmer. Add vinegar and crack the eggs into the water. Poach until the yolks are cooked to the desired degree, 3 to 5 minutes. Remove eggs with a slotted spoon, dabbing the undersides with a clean dishtowel to absorb excess water.

When you are ready to serve, set out two plates and stack the ingredients in this order: potatoes, onion and pepper mixture, chorizo, poached eggs, parmesan cheese and herbs, if using. Serve with toast.

Blueberry Bread Puddings with Maple Mascarpone

MAKES 12 MUFFIN-SIZED BREAD PUDDINGS (1 TO 2 PER SERVING)

Few dishes are more synonymous with weekend breakfast than blueberry pancakes. Sweet and succulent, blueberries are at their peak in the latter half of the summer and have a longer shelf life than other berries, making them perfect for the boating cook. We love to use blueberries from Ruby Red Farms, located on the Saanich Peninsula. In this dish, we've taken the flavours we love and used muffin tins to make individual bread puddings. It's a great way to use up a stale baguette or brioche loaf. You may also wish to try savoury combinations, such as goat's cheese and sun-dried tomatoes, or cheddar and chives.

6 eggs

2 cups (500 mL) milk

1 Tbsp (15 mL) liquid honey

1 tsp (5 mL) cinnamon

6 cups (1.4 L) stale bread cubes

1 cup (250 mL) blueberries, plus more for garnish

1 cup (250 mL) Mascarpone Cream (page 230)

Maple syrup

Preheat oven to 375F (190C). Grease muffin tins. Whisk eggs, milk, honey and cinnamon together in a medium bowl. Add bread cubes and soak for 3 to 5 minutes, depending on how stale the bread is. Cubes should be fully soaked in the egg mixture. Add blueberries and stir to combine.

Fill muffin tins with the bread pudding mixture, ensuring that the blueberries are divided well among the tins. Bake for 18 to 20 minutes or until a toothpick inserted into the centre comes out clean.

To serve, spoon a dollop of Mascarpone Cream onto each plate and create a small well using the back of a spoon. Pour maple syrup into the wells, letting some spill over the edges. Set the bread puddings beside the dollops of cream and garnish the plates with fresh blueberries.

RUBY RED FARMS

A beautiful 20-acre (8-ha) property in Deep Cove on the Saanich Peninsula is home to Ruby Red Farms, growers of certified organic blueberries. Ivan Mischenko and his now late wife, Ruby, purchased the land in 1999 with a dream of pursuing sustainable farming. Today, Ruby Red Farms is made up of 12,000 blueberry bushes—Duke and Reka varieties—that are pollinated by honeybees. Ladybugs wander over from a neighbouring farm growing beneficial insects to participate in natural pest control by hunting the aphids that roam the bushes. Picked at the peak of ripeness, Ruby Red Farms' blueberries are available fresh and frozen at Thrifty Foods and Lifestyle Markets.

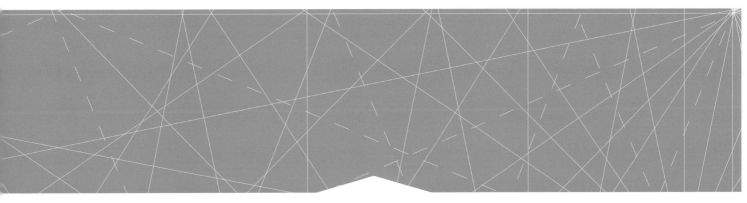

Apricot-Stuffed French Toast with Hazelnut Chocolate Spread

SERVES TWO TO FOUR

When you have leftover French bread to use up and you're looking for something sweet and decadent to prepare for brunch, this stuffed French toast fits the bill. The apricots pair nicely with a smearing of our Hazelnut Chocolate Spread (page 226). Experiment with any other fruit you may have on board.

4 slices French (or country-style) bread, cut 1¼-in (3.2-cm) thick

¼ cup (60 mL) apricot jam

4 ripe apricots, thinly sliced

4 eggs

¼ cup (60 mL) cream

Pinch of cinnamon

1 Tbsp (15 mL) butter

Hazelnut Chocolate Spread (page 226)

Slice into the top crust of each piece of bread to create a deep pocket (but do not slice all the way through). Spread apricot jam in each pocket, covering both sides of it. Stuff the pockets with as many apricot slices as will fit, reserving leftover slices for garnish. Set the stuffed bread aside.

In a shallow bowl, whisk together eggs, cream and cinnamon. One at a time, place the bread slices in the egg mixture and let soak for 30 seconds on each side, ensuring that bread is well coated but not oversaturated.

Melt butter in a medium non-stick pan over medium-high heat. Working in batches if necessary, cook the bread on both sides until golden, approximately 4 minutes a side. Remove from the pan to individual plates.

Spread a thin layer of Hazelnut Chocolate Spread on each slice of bread. Top with remaining sliced apricots and serve.

Ricotta Hotcakes

SERVES FOUR

We first tasted ricotta hotcakes on a trip to Australia and fell for their cheesecake-like flavour. When the tides aren't dictating that you get off to an early start in the morning, linger over the stove with a cup of coffee in hand. On the boat, we often use self-rising flour, which contains salt and baking powder. At home, measure the amount that you'll need for this recipe into a zippered plastic bag, if this is the only dish you will be using it for. Serve with Plum and Vanilla Bean Compote (page 221) or Blueberry, Lemon and Thyme Compote (page 223).

1½ cups (350 mL) self-rising flour

¼ cup (60 mL) granulated sugar

2 eggs

1 cup (250 mL) milk

2 Tbsp (30 mL) unsalted butter, melted

1 tsp (5 mL) lemon juice

1 cup (250 mL) ricotta cheese

1 Tbsp (15 mL) canola oil, for frying

Plum and Vanilla Bean Compote (page 221) or Blueberry, Lemon and Thyme Compote (page 223)

Combine flour and sugar in a medium bowl. In a second bowl, whisk eggs, milk, butter and lemon juice. Add wet ingredients to dry ingredients and stir until just blended. Fold in ricotta cheese. Heat canola oil in a large non-stick frying pan over medium heat. Working in batches, cook three small hotcakes at a time in the pan until golden, approximately 1 minute per side. Keep cooked hotcakes warm on a plate under foil while cooking the remaining batches.

Serve hotcakes family-style in the middle of the table, with bowls of fruit compote provided for everyone to share.

Tribune Bay Provincial Park on Hornby Island is a favourite spot to drop anchor and row ashore.
ALISON MALONE EATHORNE PHOTO

CHAPTER THREE

ON THE **BEACH**

Sailing in the Gulf Islands allows access to a great variety of beautiful beaches, marine parks and secluded anchorages, some of which are hidden gems known only to boaters. Tribune Bay, Saturna Island, Clam Bay, Glenthorne Passage and Pirates Cove are just a few of our favourites. Part of the fun is exploring the shoreline in your dinghy or kayak while looking for the perfect picnic spot. Consider packing hearty salads and artisanal-inspired sandwiches.

Farmstand Orzo Salad

SERVES SIX TO EIGHT

Fresh vegetables are star ingredients on your menu at the beginning of the trip—when you've just stocked up at the grocery store—and along the way after you've visited one of the islands' charming farmers' markets. Made with raw produce, this pasta salad is bursting with bright summer flavours. Crumbled feta cheese adds a nice salty bite.

1½ cups (350 mL) orzo

¼ cup (60 mL) Lemon Vinaigrette (page 229)

2 cups (475 mL) thinly sliced green and/or yellow zucchini rounds

1 handful snow peas

Kernels from 1 raw cob of corn, approximately ¾ cup (180 mL)

1 cup (250 mL) halved cherry tomatoes

⅓ cup (80 mL) chopped mixed herbs (we use dill, chives and parsley)

⅓ cup (80 mL) crumbled feta cheese

Cook orzo in a pot of boiling water until al dente, approximately 8 minutes. Drain. Transfer to a serving bowl and toss with the vinaigrette. Cool to room temperature. Add vegetables, herbs and feta cheese. Toss and serve.

OPPOSITE PAGE, TOP RIGHT: The Manson's Landing Market on Cortes Island offers the opportunity to replenish supplies.
JULIE BEAUREGARD–STEWART PHOTO

Layered Quinoa and Bean Salad

SERVES FOUR TO SIX

Bean salad, a summer staple in our family, is a favourite at picnic time. The choice of beans is often determined by what is available at the farmers' market. We like to use a combination of fresh, cooked and canned beans, along with English peas, for a variety of colours and textures. Light, fluffy and nutty in flavour, quinoa is the perfect complement. For a pretty presentation, layer the quinoa, beans and peas in Mason jars or other clear containers. At home, use a large glass bowl to show off the layers when serving. In this salad, we love to use the sprouting beans from Eatmore Sprouts, located in the Comox Valley.

1½ cups (350 mL) water

¼ tsp (1 mL) salt

¾ cup (180 mL) quinoa

1 cup (250 mL) chopped green beans, cut diagonally into bite-sized pieces

1 cup (250 mL) chopped yellow wax beans, cut diagonally into bite-sized pieces

1 cup (250 mL) English peas, fresh from the pods

1 × 14 fl oz (398 mL) can pinto beans, drained and rinsed

1 × 14 fl oz (398 mL) can kidney beans, drained and rinsed

1 cup (250 mL) sprouting beans

¼ cup (60 mL) Lemon Vinaigrette (page 229)

In a medium saucepan, bring the 1½ cups (350 mL) water to a boil. Add salt and quinoa. Reduce heat to low, cover and simmer for 20 minutes. Remove from heat and allow to cool.

In a small pot of boiling water, blanch green beans by cooking for 3 minutes. Remove beans to an ice bath, leaving the boiling water in the pot, and allow beans to cool for a few minutes. Drain. Repeat the process for the yellow beans.

Line up your jars and divide the quinoa among them. Add beans and peas in layers, adding the sprouting beans last. Secure the lids and transport the salads to your picnic in a cooler. When ready to serve, add Lemon Vinaigrette and shake the jars to dress the salads. Pass out forks. No plates required!

EATMORE SPROUTS & GREENS

Situated on 3¾ acres (1.5 ha) in the beautiful Comox Valley, Eatmore Sprouts & Greens began as a backyard cottage enterprise in 1975 and has been growing certified organic sprouts and greens ever since. Current owners Carmen and Glenn Wakeling produce several varieties year round, including alfalfa, garlic, deli, clover, broccoli and mixed-bean sprouts, as well as pea shoots, sunflower greens and microgreens. Produce from Eatmore Sprouts & Greens is available at Save-On Foods, Thrifty Foods, Quality Foods, IGA, Whole Foods and Planet Organic Market.

LEFT: Kayakers pass Valdes Island.
ALISON MALONE EATHORNE PHOTO

Market Summer Roll

For an inspired take on the Vietnamese summer roll, we like to roll rice paper around a combination of brightly hued, market-fresh vegetables. The ingredient quantities will depend on how many rolls you are making, so we've left that open. Plan for about 1 oz (28 gr) cooked vermicelli noodles and 3 oz (85 gr) vegetables per roll. And if counter space is limited on board, we suggest making them at home and wrapping them individually in plastic wrap for easy transport. Grilled spot prawns are delicious in these rolls, as well. Serve with your favourite peanut sauce.

Rice vermicelli noodles

Asparagus spears

Kale leaves, stems and ribs removed

Mint leaves

Rice paper sheets

Carrot, julienned

Pea shoots or sunflower sprouts

Red pepper, cut into long strips

Daikon radish, cut into long matchsticks

Bring a kettle full of water to a boil. Place noodles in a bowl and pour in enough boiling water to cover them. Cover the bowl and let the noodles cook until softened, approximately 5 minutes. Drain and allow to cool.

Blanch asparagus spears in boiling water for 2 minutes. Immediately transfer the spears to cold water to retain their bright green colour. Once cooled completely, drain and set aside.

Stack kale leaves and roll them lengthwise into one tight roll. Cut kale in chiffonade by slicing the roll thinly. Unravel the strips. Repeat the process with the mint leaves.

Fill a deep pie dish (or any deep circular dish that is wider in diameter than the rice paper sheets) with warm water. Place a rice paper sheet in the water for approximately 1 minute or until softened. Remove from the water and lay on a clean kitchen towel (it will absorb any excess water).

For each roll, stack one rice paper sheet on top of another. Lay vegetables and noodles down middle of the stacked rice paper sheets. (Do not put too many or they will be difficult to roll.) Rolling away from you, fold the sheets over the filling. Fold sides in toward the middle of the roll and wrap snugly. The rice paper will stick to itself. Repeat process for the rest of the rolls.

Chicken Salad Wrap with Apricots and Almonds

SERVES FOUR

This wrap has quickly become a family favourite. Roast the chicken at home in advance or, easier still, pick up a small roasted chicken at the grocery store before heading off on the boat. Making this wrap is also a great way of using up leftover grilled chicken from the previous night.

2 cups (475 mL) cooked and shredded chicken breast

¼ cup (60 mL) sliced dried apricots

½ cup (125 mL) sliced almonds

½ cup (125 mL) diced celery

½ cup (125 mL) sliced green onions

4 soft tortilla wraps

1 handful arugula

DRESSING

⅓ cup (80 mL) plain Greek-style yogurt

¼ cup (60 mL) mayonnaise

1 tsp (5 mL) ground cumin

1 tsp (5 mL) cinnamon

1 tsp (5 mL) chipotle powder

Juice of ½ lemon

In a large bowl, mix together the chicken, apricots, almonds, celery and green onions. Mix all of the dressing ingredients together in a small bowl. Add the dressing to the chicken mixture and toss to coat.

Lay the wraps out flat on your work surface. Spoon chicken mixture lengthwise down the middle of each one. Top with arugula and wrap firmly. Slice each chicken salad wrap in half diagonally. Take the wraps to your picnic in an airtight container.

Artisan Sandwiches, Three Ways

Pack your picnic basket with these mouth-watering sandwiches. Filled with café–inspired ingredients, they are hearty and satisfying fare on a day's outing.

CHARCUTERIE SANDWICH WITH OLIVE TAPENADE

The muffuletta sandwich is a large circular loaf filled with layers of olive salad, provolone, Swiss cheese and spicy cured meats. Traditionally, the sandwich is wrapped tightly in plastic wrap and allowed to marinate in the refrigerator for up to 24 hours to allow the flavours to meld. For our version, we suggest filling ciabatta buns with olive tapenade, along with a combination of your favourite cured meats and cheeses. Keep them wrapped snuggly until it's time to serve.

GRILLED SUMMER VEGETABLE SANDWICH WITH ARUGULA AND WALNUT PESTO

This sandwich is perfect for when you have left-over grilled vegetables from the night before. Slather rustic olive bread with Arugula and Walnut Pesto (page 218) and top with grilled vegetables and goat's cheese.

SERRANO HAM, BLUE CHEESE AND PEAR

Cured Serrano ham is an excellent choice for the boater's lunch menu. Pair it with soft blue cheese (such as You Boo Blue from Hilary's Cheese), along with beautifully ripe pear and peppery arugula for a delightful sandwich.

SANDWICHES

Sandwiches are quintessential picnic fare. Whether you're eating lunch while underway or packing up your dinghy for a day of exploring on shore, it's nice to have a hand-held lunch that is both hearty and rich in flavour. For the most part, exact measurements aren't required. Instead, we have provided a few suggestions for interesting combinations that might broaden your sandwich repertoire. In some cases, we've suggested specific breads that complement the sandwich filling. However it's often simply a matter of choosing your favourite, whether it's a crusty ciabatta bun, a beautiful demi-baguette, a rustic olive loaf, artisan sourdough or rosemary focaccia. Tortilla wraps and flatbreads have a long shelf life and are excellent options for extended cruises.

Spot Prawn and Avocado Roll

SERVES FOUR

Inspired by east coast lobster rolls, we created this sandwich to showcase spot prawns, the succulent crustaceans that are in season on the West Coast for six to eight weeks every spring, usually beginning in early May. Of the shrimp species harvested off Canada's west coast, spot prawns are the largest—and most delicious. If you're making this sandwich outside of spot prawn season, consider using local side stripes.

1 lemon, cut in half

1 lb (454 gr) spot prawns, peeled and deveined

¼ cup (60 mL) mayonnaise

1 Tbsp (15 mL) each coarsely chopped flat-leaf parsley, dill and chives

Dash of hot sauce

Salt and pepper

4 soft white rolls, cut open

1 avocado, halved and sliced into long pieces

Fill a small saucepan with water. Bring to a simmer over medium heat. Add a pinch of salt and one half of the lemon. Drop in the prawns. Poach until pink and firm, approximately 3 minutes. Drain and allow to cool to room temperature.

In a large bowl, whisk the juice of the remaining half a lemon with mayonnaise, herbs and hot sauce. Gently fold in the prawns. Season to taste with salt and pepper.

Stuff the rolls with the prawn mixture and top with avocado slices. Take the rolls to your picnic in an airtight container.

TRUE GRAIN BREAD

Dock your boat in Cowichan Bay and stroll up to True Grain Bread, a charming bakery that handcrafts organic bread and pastries. Established in 2004 by Jonathan Knight, the business is now owned by Bruce and Leslie Stewart, an Ontario couple who take pride in baking with traditional methods. Whole and sifted grains—including heritage Red Fife and ancient kamut, spelt and emmer—are milled on site using an authentic Austrian stone mill. In addition to the original Cowichan Bay location, True Grain Bread now has stores in Mill Bay and in Summerland, in BC's southern interior.

Chunky Salmon-Salad Sandwich with Horseradish, Apple and Bacon

SERVES FOUR

This hearty sandwich is filled with seared salmon filet, spicy horseradish, tart grated apple and smoky bacon—an unexpected combination that delivers in spades. If you haven't cooked the bacon at home ahead of time and doing so on board is not practical for you, we suggest substituting it with a light smear of Bacon Jam (page 220) on each sandwich.

8 strips bacon

1½ lbs (681 gr) salmon filet

Salt and pepper

1 Tbsp (15 mL) olive oil

4 Tbsp (60 mL) mayonnaise

2 tsp (10 mL) grainy mustard

2 tsp (10 mL) horseradish

1 tsp (5 mL) liquid honey

½ apple, grated

1 baguette

Butter

4 large leaves butter lettuce

In a medium non-stick pan, cook bacon until crisp and golden. Drain on paper towels and set aside.

Season salmon filet with salt and pepper. Pour olive oil into a medium non-stick pan and warm over medium heat. Add filet, skin side down. Pan-fry salmon uncovered, turning once, until it is just cooked, approximately 6 minutes. Remove from heat and allow to cool to room temperature.

In a medium bowl, combine mayonnaise, mustard, horseradish, honey and grated apple. Season to taste with salt and pepper. Gently flake salmon into large chunks and fold into mayonnaise mixture.

Cut the baguette into four and slice the pieces open. Lightly butter the bottoms, and top with salmon salad, bacon and lettuce. Close up the sandwiches and wrap them in parchment paper; store in the refrigerator or cooler until lunchtime.

Lavender Shortbread

MAKES 16 SQUARES

Lavender, a beautifully fragrant plant that grows profusely in flower beds on Vancouver Island, adds lovely floral, lemony notes to traditional shortbread. There are several varieties that provide great visual appeal, but the buds of the English lavender, Lavandula angustifolia, are the lightest and most fragrant, and the most suitable for cooking. We recommend that you purchase buds designated for culinary use from a local lavender farm or specialty food store. This delicious shortbread makes a perfect portable snack.

1 cup (250 mL) unsalted butter, chilled and cut in small cubes

⅔ cup (160 mL) granulated sugar

½ tsp (2.5 mL) salt

2 Tbsp (30 mL) dried lavender buds, ground in the food processor or with a mortar and pestle

2 cups (475 mL) all-purpose flour

⅔ cup (160 mL) cornstarch

2 Tbsp (30 mL) fine berry sugar

Preheat oven to 325F (160C). Line an 8-in (20-cm) square baking pan with parchment paper.

Mix butter, granulated sugar, salt and lavender in the bowl of a food processor. Add flour and cornstarch and mix until well blended. Press dough evenly into the baking pan. Bake for 30 minutes or until the edges are light brown.

Remove shortbread from the oven and sprinkle berry sugar overtop. Cool partially and cut into 16 squares. When completely cooled, remove from pan and store in an airtight container.

CHAPTER FOUR

FRESH

Southern Vancouver Island and the Gulf Islands are the perfect weekend getaway destinations. Set sail from Sidney, fill your basket with fresh produce at the Saturday farmers' market in Ganges and drop anchor in Montague Harbour. After a late afternoon swim off the white-shell beach, prepare dinner on the barbecue with a glass of locally crafted beer or cider in hand.

Whether you are a novice or seasoned fisherman, there's something very satisfying about catching dinner. If you aren't feeling so lucky, you can stroll the public wharf, on the lookout for a fishing boat with fresh catch on offer. And before you drop your hook or bait your trap, it is important to be aware of the issues relating to sustainable seafood. Ocean Wise, a Vancouver Aquarium initiative, is a good resource for our coast.

Grilled Spot Prawns with Chili Vinaigrette

SERVES FOUR AS AN APPETIZER

On the West Coast, May to June is spot prawn season. While they are widely available at grocery stores, fish markets and directly from boats docked in the harbour, there's nothing better than eating spot prawns that you've plucked from the waters beneath your hull. We first caught spot prawns in the Broughton Archipelago, the largest marine park in British Columbia. Following an afternoon spent kayaking amid the jewel-like islets, we returned to our boat, pulled up the trap and were pleasantly surprised to find it full of the large, coral-hued beauties.

1 lb (454 gr) fresh spot prawns, shells and tails on (approximately 25 to 35 spot prawns)

2½ Tbsp (37 mL) extra-virgin olive oil

2 cloves garlic, finely minced

½ tsp (2.5 mL) red pepper flakes

2 Tbsp (30 mL) white wine

Salt and pepper

1 lemon, cut into wedges

Soak a few wooden skewers in water for 20 minutes. This will prevent the skewers from burning on the barbecue.

Butterfly prawns along the backs with a sharp paring knife, leaving the shells and tails on. Devein the prawns. Thread prawns lengthwise on skewers and place them in a long shallow dish.

Heat olive oil in a small saucepan over medium heat and add garlic and red pepper flakes. Sauté for 1 minute, then allow to cool to room temperature. Add white wine. Pour this marinade over the prawns and season with salt and pepper. Refrigerate for 30 minutes.

Heat the barbecue to high. Grill prawns, brushing with marinade from the bowl, until bright pink and just opaque in the centre, approximately 2 minutes per side. Remove from the skewers and transfer to a bowl or platter. Serve with lemon wedges.

Warm Potato Salad with Arugula and Walnut Pesto

SERVES SIX

In our take on potato salad, we've opted to serve it warm and have replaced the classic mayonnaise-based dressing with a beautiful pesto made from walnuts and peppery arugula. Make the pesto at home and simply toss it with the warm potatoes once you're at sea.

8 slices pancetta

3½ lbs (1.6 kg) new potatoes

3 large eggs

Arugula and Walnut Pesto (page 218)

1 cup (250 mL) arugula, lightly packed

¼ cup (60 mL) parmesan cheese shavings

Preheat oven to 350F (175C). Lay the slices of pancetta on a rimmed baking sheet and bake, turning once, until crisp, approximately 6 minutes each per side.

Bring a large pot of salted water to a boil. Cook potatoes over medium heat until a knife inserted into a potato comes out easily, approximately 15 minutes. Do not overcook. During this time, cook eggs in the same pot as the potatoes for 8 minutes. Remove cooked eggs from the pot and immerse in cold water to stop the cooking process.

Drain the potatoes, then cut them in half. In a large bowl, toss the potatoes with the pesto. Let the potatoes rest for a few minutes to allow them to soak up the pesto.

When ready to serve, break pancetta slices into shards and scatter over the potatoes. Add arugula and toss. Peel eggs, cut them in half and lay them face up on top of the salad. Sprinkle parmesan cheese shavings on top.

Panzanella Caprese

SERVES FOUR

Inspired by two of our favourite Italian salads, this mixture of grilled bread, ripe tomatoes, creamy buffalo mozzarella and fresh herbs is a summer staple.

½ baguette (fresh or day-old)

¼ cup (60 mL) extra-virgin olive oil

2 large tomatoes, roughly chopped

1 small handful basil leaves, roughly torn

1 small handful flat-leaf parsley, roughly torn

½ cup (125 mL) caper berries

Salt and pepper

1 large ball buffalo mozzarella

 Cut baguette into 1-in (2.5-cm) slices and drizzle with olive oil. Grill the slices on the barbecue on both sides until the bread is toasted and has grill marks, 2 to 3 minutes per side. Tear the grilled bread into bite-sized chunks and put the pieces in a large bowl. Add tomatoes, basil, parsley and caper berries. Season to taste with a scattering of sea salt and freshly ground black pepper. Toss and transfer to a serving plate.

Tear mozzarella into rough pieces and scatter them over the salad. Drizzle with olive oil. Let the salad rest for 10 minutes before serving to allow the bread to soak up juice from the tomatoes.

WASTE NOT, WANT NOT: WHAT TO DO WITH DAY-OLD BREAD

Picking up a fresh, fragrant loaf of bread at a charming bakery is one of life's greatest pleasures. Unless you're feeding a crowd, however, you're likely to end up with leftovers. At home, most of us toss extra bits and pieces into the freezer to be used for stuffing a turkey at Thanksgiving or Christmas. When we're far from land, we like to find inventive ways to use up day-old or stale bread.

- sliced and grilled for crostini, pages 123 and 127
- tossed with tomatoes for a Tuscan-inspired bread salad, page 90

- baked with an egg mixture in muffin tins for sweet and savoury bread puddings, page 64
- stuffed and dipped in eggs for French toast, page 66
- grilled cheese sandwiches, page 161
- cubed, tossed in olive oil, salt and pepper, and toasted in a sauté pan for crunchy croutons
- toast thick slices of bread, rub them with a garlic clove and top with a drizzle of olive oil and a scattering of sea salt for garlic toast
- stale pitas can be toasted and tossed into a fattoush-inspired salad with cucumber, tomato, red onion and herbs

UNTAMED FEAST

Foraging for wild food takes patience, perseverance and a deep knowledge base. These qualities can all be found in Eric Whitehead, creator and head harvester of Untamed Feast, who began foraging in 1999. Based in the Cowichan Valley, his company specializes in gourmet wild mushrooms, including morel, porcini, lobster, chanterelle, hedgehog and pine varieties. Every spring and fall, Whitehead hand harvests these well-known edible species—which cannot be farmed or cultivated—from remote forests in Haida Gwaii and farther afield in BC; he also ventures to Alberta and the Northwest Territories. The day they are picked, the mushrooms are dried in a mobile food drier and immediately packaged in high-barrier food-grade plastic bags. In addition to the line of pure dried mushrooms—which are rich in concentrated flavour—Untamed Feast produces preservative-free mixes for mushroom gravy and mushroom soup, and three mushroom and rice dish mixes (which contain wild nettle that Whitehead harvests himself). Untamed Feast products are available at Whole Foods, Choices and Planet Organic Market.

Wild Rice and Mushroom Soup

SERVES SIX

Vancouver Island is home to a rich variety of wild mushroom species. In this recipe, we've combined earthy chanterelles, black trumpets and morels with nutty Canadian wild rice. On a chilly night, having a pot of this soup simmering on the stove is nothing short of restorative. Whenever we can, we use the beautiful dried wild mushrooms from Untamed Feast, based in the Cowichan Valley.

½ cup (125 mL) wild rice

1½ cups (350 mL) water

2 Tbsp (30 mL) butter

1.4 oz (40 gr) dried wild mushrooms

4 slices bacon, diced (or 1 Tbsp/15 mL Bacon Jam, page 220)

1 onion, chopped

2 cloves garlic, minced

2 cups (475 mL) mixed fresh mushrooms, sliced (we use chanterelles, trumpets and morels)

2 Tbsp (30 mL) all-purpose flour

⅓ cup (80 mL) red wine

4 cups (1 L) beef stock

1 bay leaf

1 tsp (5 mL) thyme leaves

1 cup (250 mL) whipping cream

Salt and pepper

Rinse rice under cold running water using a fine sieve.

Bring water, rice and butter to a boil in a small saucepan. Cover, reduce heat to a simmer and cook until rice is just tender, approximately 30 minutes. Remove from heat and set aside.

While the rice is cooking, pour 1½ cups (350 mL) hot water over the dried mushrooms in a small bowl and let them rehydrate for at least 20 minutes. Remove mushrooms, reserving the soaking water, and roughly chop.

Crisp bacon in a large saucepan. Remove bacon from the pan, leaving the bacon fat, and drain on paper towels. Add onions to reserved bacon fat and cook over low heat until softened, approximately 3 minutes. Add garlic and cook until just fragrant, approximately 30 seconds. Add fresh mushrooms and cook for an additional 5 minutes. Add rehydrated mushrooms.

Stir in flour and cook for 2 minutes. Add red wine, beef stock and reserved mushroom soaking water, pouring in a slow stream, followed by bay leaf, thyme, cooked rice and whipping cream. Season to taste with salt and pepper.

Simmer over low heat for 15 minutes. Remove bay leaf and serve immediately.

Grilled Harissa Chicken with Cucumber and Red Onion Salad

SERVES FOUR TO SIX

Marinated in our Harissa Spice Paste (page 225) and thick Greek-style yogurt, this spicy chicken stays wonderfully moist when cooked on the grill. We love to serve it wrapped in warm flatbread with cool yogurt and a refreshing salad of cucumber, parsley, mint and red onion.

GRILLED HARISSA CHICKEN

1 Tbsp (15 mL) Harissa Spice Paste (page 225)

¼ cup (60 mL) plain Greek-style yogurt

4 boneless, skinless chicken thighs

2 boneless, skinless chicken breasts

CUCUMBER AND RED ONION SALAD

1 small English cucumber

¼ cup (60 mL) coarsely chopped flat-leaf parsley

2 Tbsp (30 mL) coarsely chopped fresh mint

½ red onion, thinly sliced

2 Tbsp (30 mL) extra-virgin olive oil

Juice of ½ lemon

Salt and pepper

TO SERVE

4–6 flatbreads

GRILLED HARISSA CHICKEN In a large plastic container with a tight-fitting lid, combine Harissa Spice Paste with plain yogurt. Add chicken and coat evenly with the yogurt mixture. Refrigerate in the sealed container for 1 to 2 hours to allow the chicken to marinate.

Preheat barbecue to medium. Grill the chicken pieces for 8 to 10 minutes on each side, until they are completely cooked and juices run clear. Keep an eye on the chicken to prevent burning. Remove chicken from the grill and cover with foil. Let rest for 5 to 10 minutes before serving.

CUCUMBER AND RED ONION SALAD With a vegetable peeler, shave the cucumber into long strips. Toss with herbs, onions, olive oil and lemon juice. Season to taste with salt and pepper.

TO SERVE Warm flatbreads on the barbecue for 1 minute per side. Serve chicken, salad, yogurt and flatbreads family-style so that everyone may assemble their own wraps.

Grilled Summer Vegetables

SERVES TWO

When the barbecue is hot for grilling meat, the no-fuss way to cook the accompanying vegetables is on the grill as well. They can be roasted on the open grill or cooked on foil—or both ways, which is our preference. Cooking vegetables on the grill imparts a true roasted flavour, while finishing them off on foil retains the juices, keeping the veggies naturally flavourful. However you do it, cooking vegetables on a hot barbecue is quick and easy and eliminates the need to wash a roasting pan.

This summer mix includes zucchini, tomatoes, onions, mushrooms, fennel and eggplant, but the options are endless. You may wish to try red and yellow peppers or asparagus. Leftovers work well in the next day's pasta, bean or rice salad, or Grilled Summer Vegetable Sandwich (page 77). Our recipe for Grilled Root Vegetables is on page 144.

1 small zucchini, cut into 1-in (2.5-cm) slices

6 cherry tomatoes, whole

½ sweet white onion, cut into 1-in (2.5-cm) slices

1 cup (250 mL) halved mushrooms

2 fennel bulbs, sliced (core removed)

1 small eggplant, cut into 1-in (2.5-cm) slices

2 cloves garlic, minced

2 Tbsp (30 mL) olive oil

1 sprig thyme, leaves removed

1 tsp (5 mL) dried oregano

Salt and pepper

1 small handful basil leaves, roughly torn

Toss all vegetables except the cherry tomatoes in a bowl with oil and herbs. Season with salt and pepper. Lay the vegetable slices on the grill and cook over medium-high heat for 2 minutes on each side. Transfer to a piece of heavy foil on the grill, adding tomatoes. Cook until tender. Garnish with fresh basil.

Halibut Tacos with Red Cabbage and Cilantro Slaw and Avocado Cream

SERVES FOUR (MAKES 12 SMALL TACOS)

We once made this dish while anchored in Tribune Bay off Hornby Island. It was one of those blissfully warm August evenings where everything was as it should be. After an early evening plunge in the sparkling, turquoise water, we sipped ice-cold Beachcomber Summer Ale from Vancouver Island Brewery while preparing our meal. Summer at its best.

In this recipe, the dry rub on the halibut creates a spicy crust. The red cabbage and cilantro slaw and lime-infused avocado cream enhance the fish with their bright flavours.

HALIBUT

½ tsp (2.5 mL) salt

1 tsp (5 mL) fresh thyme leaves

¼ tsp (1 mL) dried oregano

¼ tsp (1 mL) cayenne

½ tsp (2.5 mL) sweet smoked paprika

½ tsp (2.5 mL) black pepper

¼ tsp (1 mL) fennel seeds, crushed

¼ tsp (1 mL) onion powder

1½ lbs (681 gr) halibut filets, skin removed

RED CABBAGE AND CILANTRO SLAW

1 tsp (5 mL) liquid honey

½ tsp (2.5 mL) ground cumin

Juice of 1 lime

¼ cup (60 mL) canola oil

Salt and pepper

2 cups (475 mL) shredded red cabbage

⅓ cup (80 mL) shredded red onion

⅓ cup (80 mL) roughly chopped cilantro

HALIBUT ⤳ Preheat oven to 350F (175C). Combine the herbs and spices (not including the cilantro) in a bowl. Coat halibut with this dry rub. Bake until firm to the touch, approximately 10 to 12 minutes. Remove from oven and keep warm under foil.

RED CABBAGE AND CILANTRO SLAW ⤳ In a large bowl, combine honey, cumin, lime juice and canola oil. Season to taste with salt and pepper. Toss in cabbage, onions and cilantro. Set the slaw aside.

. . . CONTINUED ON NEXT PAGE

AVOCADO CREAM

½ cup (125 mL) sour cream

Juice of 1 lime

1 Tbsp (15 mL) each chopped cilantro, mint
and flat-leaf parsley

⅓ cup (80 mL) olive oil

1 large avocado, pitted and peeled

Salt and pepper

TO ASSEMBLE

12 small corn tortillas

1 small handful cilantro, for garnish

AVOCADO CREAM In a deep bowl, pulse ingredients together with an immersion blender. If you don't have an immersion blender, mash avocado with a fork and whisk in the other ingredients.

TO ASSEMBLE Warm corn tortillas in a frying pan or in the oven. Flake the halibut. Fill each tortilla with halibut, slaw and avocado cream and top with cilantro.

VANCOUVER ISLAND BREWERY

A passion for microbrewing is what sparked the birth of award-winning Vancouver Island Brewery, British Columbia's oldest independently operated brewery. Spearheaded by Cobble Hill farmer Barry Fischer, a group of local residents with a shared dream of opening the island's first craft brewery launched their company in 1984 in a small Central Saanich warehouse; a flourishing business led the team to open their downtown Victoria location in 1995. Vancouver Island Brewery produces a wide variety of all-natural handcrafted beers, including seasonal favourites such as Beachcomber Summer Ale and Storm Watcher Winter Lager. Over 80 percent of the brewery's beer is sold on Vancouver Island, the remainder being sold across BC. Vancouver Island Brewery's world-class beers are available at both government and private liquor stores.

Albacore Tuna Burgers with Pickled Cucumber and Wasabi Mayo

SERVES FOUR

This recipe showcases premium-quality wild albacore tuna, locally caught and flash frozen at sea. When we first made these burgers, we noticed a tracing number on the processor's packaging that allowed us to trace where, when and how the fish was caught. We were pleased to learn that our tuna was caught off Ucluelet, a town on the west coast of the island. Taking only minutes to cook, this burger is a nice, light addition to the boating burger roster.

PICKLED CUCUMBER

1 small English cucumber, peeled and thinly sliced

¼ cup (125 mL) thinly sliced Vidalia onion

1 tsp (5 mL) dried dill

½ tsp (2.5 mL) granulated sugar

2 Tbsp (30 mL) white wine vinegar

Salt and pepper

WASABI MAYO

1 Tbsp (15 mL) wasabi paste

¼ cup (60 mL) plus 1½ tsp (7.5 mL) mayonnaise

TUNA BURGERS

1 lb (454 gr) small wild albacore tuna loins

2 Tbsp (30 mL) canola oil

Salt and pepper

4 ciabatta buns, toasted

1 avocado, sliced

Pea shoots (or other sprouts)

PICKLED CUCUMBER Combine all ingredients in a bowl and let sit for 15 minutes before using.

WASABI MAYO Combine wasabi and mayonnaise in a small bowl.

TUNA BURGERS Coat the sides of the tuna loins using 1 Tbsp (15 mL) canola oil. Season all sides with salt and pepper.

In a sauté pan over medium-high heat, sear tuna loins in the remaining 1 Tbsp (15 mL) canola oil for 2 minutes on each side, ensuring that outsides have a uniform crust (insides will still be rare). Remove tuna from the pan and let rest for 5 minutes. Slice tuna into ½-in (1.3-cm) slices.

Spread wasabi mayo on bottom half of each bun. Top with tuna, pickled cucumber, avocado and pea shoots.

Herbed Ling Cod Cakes with Crisp Potato Rösti and Caper Rémoulade

SERVES SIX

Our boating-friendly version of fish and chips, this dish is fun to prepare at the end of a leisurely day. If you have fish left over from last night's dinner, this is a great way to put it to use. Alternatively, the cod cakes taste great with greens on ciabatta buns.

CAPER RÉMOULADE

1 cup (250 mL) mayonnaise

1 tsp (5 mL) Dijon mustard

1 Tbsp (15 mL) chopped capers

1 tsp (5 mL) gherkin pickle juice

1 Tbsp (15 mL) chopped gherkin pickles

Zest and juice of ½ lemon

1 Tbsp (15 mL) minced flat-leaf parsley

1 Tbsp (15 mL) minced dill

Salt and pepper

LING COD CAKES

1½ lbs (681 gr) ling cod filets

2 cups (475 mL) panko bread crumbs

2 Tbsp (30 mL) chopped chives

2 Tbsp (30 mL) chopped flat-leaf parsley

Zest of 1 lemon

1 tsp (5 mL) olive oil

2 cloves garlic, minced

1 egg

2 tsp (10 mL) all-purpose flour

¼ cup (60 mL) mayonnaise

Salt and pepper

2 Tbsp (30 mL) canola oil, for frying

CAPER RÉMOULADE Stir together all ingredients in a small bowl.

LING COD CAKES In a 350F (175C) oven, bake cod on a baking sheet until cooked through and easily flaked, approximately 6 to 10 minutes. Remove from oven and cool. Break into small pieces.

In a medium bowl, mix together the panko, herbs, lemon zest, olive oil, garlic, egg, flour and mayonnaise. Add the cod and stir to combine. Season to taste with salt and pepper. Form the mixture into six round cakes. Heat canola oil in a large sauté pan. Fry cod cakes over medium-high heat until crisp, approximately 4 minutes per side. Remove from the pan and keep warm on a plate under foil.

. . . CONTINUED ON NEXT PAGE

CRISP POTATO RÖSTI

3 russet potatoes, peeled and grated

1 onion, grated

Juice of ½ lemon

1 tsp (5 mL) onion powder

⅓ cup (80 mL) all-purpose flour

Salt and pepper

2 Tbsp (30 mL) canola oil, for frying

GARNISH

1 small handful frisée or sprouts

CRISP POTATO RÖSTI ◠ Rinse potatoes in cold water and pat dry with a kitchen towel. Combine with onion in a large bowl. Stir in lemon juice. Add onion powder and flour. Season with salt and pepper. Mix well. Form the mixture into six discs.

Heat canola oil in a sauté pan. Cook potato rösti over medium-high heat until crisp, approximately 7 minutes per side. Drain on paper towels.

TO SERVE ◠ Set one potato rösti on each plate. Top with a cod cake and caper rémoulade. Garnish with frisée or sprouts. ◞

TOP LEFT: Finn, our English Springer Spaniel, enjoys an afternoon swim.

Spiced Lamb Burgers with Lemon and Dill Yogurt

SERVES SIX

When the days are sunny and the evenings are long, boaters love to prepare dinner at the grill. This recipe is a go-to when we want to serve a casual meal that goes above and beyond the standard burger. Serve with Polenta Fries (page 108).

1 small white onion, finely chopped

1 × 1-in (2.5-cm) piece fresh ginger, peeled and minced

3 cloves garlic, minced

¼ cup (60 mL) coarsely chopped cilantro (stalks and leaves)

1 green chili, seeds removed and finely chopped

2 Tbsp (30 mL) olive oil

2 lbs (908 gr) ground lamb

1½ tsp (7.5 mL) ground cumin

2 tsp (10 mL) garam masala

1 tsp (5 mL) salt

½ tsp (2.5 mL) black pepper

1 large egg

⅓ cup (80 mL) panko (or regular) bread crumbs

1 small red onion, sliced into rings

1 Tbsp (15 mL) butter

6 ciabatta buns, sliced open

2–3 plum tomatoes, sliced

6–10 lettuce leaves

¾ cup (180 mL) Lemon and Dill Yogurt (page 228)

Sauté white onions, ginger, garlic, cilantro and green chilies in 1 Tbsp (15 mL) of the olive oil. Remove from heat. Once cool, add lamb, cumin, garam masala, salt, pepper, egg and panko. Mix gently by hand and do not overwork. Shape into burger patties that are roughly the same circumference as the buns. Chill patties for 30 minutes.

Preheat barbecue to medium-high heat. Sauté rings of red onion in butter and the remaining 1 Tbsp (15 mL) olive oil over medium heat until soft, approximately 5 minutes. Keep warm in the pan. Grill lamb patties on both sides on a well-oiled grill, cooking all the way through, approximately 12 minutes total. Toast the ciabatta buns. When you assemble the burgers, top the lamb patties with tomato slices, lettuce, sautéed onions and Lemon and Dill Yogurt.

Polenta Fries with Smoked Paprika Aioli

SERVES FOUR

When you get together with friends, impress them with these amazing "fries." Serve them with Smoked Paprika Aioli (page 231) and everyone will wonder which specialty food store you visited just before dropping anchor.

1¼ cups (300 mL) polenta (fine cornmeal)

3 cups (710 mL) water

Pinch of salt

2 Tbsp (30 mL) butter

¾ cup (180 mL) finely grated parmesan cheese

3 sprigs thyme, leaves removed

1 cup (250 mL) Smoked Paprika Aioli (page 231)

Combine 1 cup (250 mL) polenta with the water and salt in a medium saucepan. Bring to a boil and then reduce to a simmer, stirring frequently. Continue simmering for 10 minutes. Add butter and ½ cup (125 mL) of parmesan cheese. Stir to combine and remove from heat. Grease an 8-in (20-cm) square baking pan. Pour in polenta. Let cool for 30 minutes or until set enough for slicing.

Preheat oven to 400F (205C). Cut the polenta into 24 rectangular fries. Transfer the fries from the pan to a bowl. Combine thyme, the remaining ¼ cup (60 mL) polenta and the remaining ¼ cup (60 mL) parmesan cheese. Tossing gently, coat the fries in the mixture. Transfer the fries to an oiled baking sheet. Bake, turning frequently to brown all sides, for approximately 20 minutes.

As an alternative to baking the fries in the oven, you can cook them on a barbecue. Preheat barbecue to medium-high heat. Brush all sides of the fries with olive oil before tossing in the parmesan and thyme mixture (omit additional polenta). Grill for 10 minutes, rotating to evenly brown all sides.

Serve immediately with Smoked Paprika Aioli.

GARDEN FRESH

Few things are more evocative of summer than a fresh bouquet of flowers from a farmers' market or roadside stand. Often the mix is a potpourri of flowers, whatever happens to be in the farmer's garden that day. The bouquets are often a riot of colour, something you are not likely to find throughout the year at your neighbourhood florist. We find that flowers are good for the soul and can lift our spirits instantly.

Grilled Salmon with Tamari Soba Noodles

SERVES FOUR

Whether you are skilled enough to catch a salmon, or you purchase it from a fish shop or fishing boat, this is a great recipe to have in your boating repertoire. This Asian-inspired dish may be served warm as indicated in the recipe or cold as a summer salad. If you are in a remote location without access to a fish shop, replace the salmon filets with locally processed canned smoked salmon. The sauce may be prepared in advance and kept refrigerated. Bring to room temperature before using.

4 salmon filets, each about 6 oz (170 gr)

1 Tbsp (15 mL) canola oil

8 oz (226 gr) soba noodles (Japanese-style buckwheat noodles)

1 Tbsp (15 mL) freshly grated ginger

2 cloves garlic, minced

½ tsp (2.5 mL) red pepper flakes

4 green onions, finely chopped, plus more (sliced diagonally) for garnish

Sesame seeds (optional)

TAMARI DRESSING

2 Tbsp (30 mL) extra-virgin olive oil

1 Tbsp (15 mL) lime juice

1 Tbsp (15 mL) tamari (or soy sauce)

1 Tbsp (15 mL) fish sauce

2 Tbsp (30 mL) white wine

Pinch of granulated sugar

Preheat barbecue to medium-high heat. Lightly brush salmon filets with canola oil. Cook filets until they just begin to flake when tested with a fork, approximately 4 minutes on each side. Remove from the barbecue. Remove the crisp skin from the filets (it can later be added to side of the plate for garnish).

Meanwhile, bring a pot of water to a boil. Add soba noodles and cook for 4 to 5 minutes, until tender. Drain and rinse in warm water, then leave in pot.

Gently stir in ginger, garlic, pepper flakes and finely chopped green onions. Combine tamari dressing ingredients. Mix well and pour over the noodles. Turn the heat on to low and stir to combine. Divide noodles among four plates. Top each serving with a salmon filet and garnish with additional green onions, salmon skin and sesame seeds, if using.

Crab Spaghettini with Chili, Lemon and Basil

SERVES TWO

In anticipation of a boiled crab dinner for two, you bait your trap. Sadly, your day's catch results in one lonely crustacean. Do not despair. One crab is all that is needed for two delicious servings of this simple spaghettini dish.

5 oz (141 gr) spaghettini

¼ cup (60 mL) olive oil

1 red chili, seeded and diced

1 clove garlic, thinly sliced

Meat from 1 cooked crab (approximately 1 cup/250 mL crabmeat)

Zest and juice of 1 lemon

1 small handful basil leaves, torn

Bring a large pot of salted water to a boil. Add spaghettini to the water and cook until al dente, approximately 6 to 8 minutes. Drain pasta, reserving ½ cup (125 mL) of the cooking water.

Heat olive oil in a sauté pan. Add chilies and garlic and toss for 30 seconds or until fragrant. Toss in crabmeat, lemon zest and lemon juice.

Stirring gently, add enough reserved cooking water to the pan to create a light sauce. Add basil and toss. Serve immediately.

SATURNA ISLAND FAMILY ESTATE WINERY

Set on 78 acres (32 ha) overlooking Plumper Sound, the Pender Islands and the San Juan Islands, Saturna Island Family Estate Winery is a dream destination for the Gulf Island boater. The award-winning waterfront winery encourages visitors to drop anchor, paddle to Saturna Beach and wander up to the tasting room and bistro housed in a wood-framed barn. Established between 1995 and 2000, the winery's four vineyards sit at the base of Mount Warburton Pike, named after a British explorer who purchased 784 acres (317 ha) of land on the island in 1884. Here, pinot gris, chardonnay, gewürztraminer and pinot noir grape varietals absorb heat reflected from a large sandstone cliff before being processed in the winery building. Satura Island Family Estate Winery's products are sold at Liquor Plus stores in Victoria, Saanich, Cobble Hill and Duncan and other private liquor stores and wine shops.

Manila Clam Linguine with Cherry Tomatoes

SERVES FOUR

Clam digging is a favourite pastime for many boaters. This simple recipe punctuates the flavour of Manila clams with garlic and anchovy paste. Serve with a glass of chilled pinot gris from Saturna Island Family Estate Winery.

14 oz (397 g) linguine

2 lbs (908 gr) Manila clams, scrubbed clean

3 Tbsp (45 mL) extra-virgin olive oil

3 cloves garlic, finely minced

½ tsp (2.5 mL) anchovy paste

Salt and pepper

1 tsp (5 mL) red pepper flakes

10 cherry tomatoes, quartered

Pinch of granulated sugar

1 cup (250 mL) white wine

⅓ cup (80 mL) coarsely chopped flat-leaf parsley

Put a large pot of well-salted water on to boil. Add pasta to the boiling water and cook until al dente, approximately 8 to 10 minutes. Drain pasta, reserving ½ cup (125 mL) of the cooking water.

Sort through cleaned clams and sharply tap any that are open. Discard any that do not close.

Put olive oil into a hot sauté pan large enough to hold the clams and add garlic, anchovy paste and a pinch of both salt and pepper. Add red pepper flakes, tomatoes and sugar.

Just as the garlic begins to colour and the anchovy paste has melted, add white wine and clams. Cook with lid on for 4 minutes or until clams have opened. Add parsley and cooked pasta, stirring to combine. Gradually add just enough of the reserved cooking water to create a light sauce. Discard any clams that are still closed.

Remove from heat and serve immediately.

OPPOSITE PAGE, TOP: The community of Sointula on Malcolm Island is a favourite stopover for boats that cruise to the north end of Vancouver Island. JULIE BEAUREGARD-STEWART PHOTO. BOTTOM: Saturna Island Family Estate Winery overlooks Plumper Sound. ANDREA JOHNSON PHOTO

Lamb Chops with English Pea and Mint Mash

SERVES TWO

A play on the classic British combination of lamb and mint jelly, this dish highlights sweet, farm-fresh peas and beautifully flavoured lamb from Ruckle Heritage Farm on Salt Spring Island. Vibrantly green and wonderfully creamy, this mash is a quick-cooking substitute for mashed potatoes.

LAMB CHOPS

1 tsp (5 mL) Dijon mustard

Juice of 1 lemon

1 clove garlic, minced

¼ cup (60 mL) olive oil

Salt and pepper

4 lamb chops, each 2–3 oz (56–85 gr)

ENGLISH PEA AND MINT MASH

2½ cups (600 mL) shelled fresh English peas

1 shallot, minced

1 clove garlic, minced

1 Tbsp (15 mL) extra-virgin olive oil, plus more for garnish

1 Tbsp (15 mL) chopped fresh mint, plus more for garnish

¼ cup (60 mL) cream

Salt and pepper

LAMB CHOPS Create marinade by whisking mustard, lemon juice, garlic and olive oil in a shallow container with a tight-fitting lid. Season with salt and pepper. Place lamb chops in the container and turn to coat in marinade. Refrigerate sealed container for 30 minutes. Cook over a hot grill for 3 to 5 minutes a side, or to preferred level of doneness (5 minutes a side for well done).

ENGLISH PEA AND MINT MASH Blanch peas in boiling water for 2 minutes. Shock in ice-cold water to retain vivid green colour. Sauté shallots and garlic in olive oil in a large pan over medium-high heat. Add peas and cook for 3 minutes or until just tender. Add mint and cream and mix well. Mash peas with a potato masher. Season to taste with salt and pepper.

Serve lamb chops atop pea mash on individual plates. Garnish with fresh mint and a drizzle of good-quality extra-virgin olive oil.

RUCKLE HERITAGE FARM

Set on 200 bucolic acres (80 ha) on Salt Spring Island, Ruckle Heritage Farm has a rich history dating back to 1872. It was that year when Henry Ruckle, one of the island's earliest settlers, arrived on Salt Spring in search of farmland. Ruckle purchased land on the island's lower-end peninsula and over the years grew it into a large-scale operation that at one time included 600 fruit trees, 40 nut trees, a variety of livestock and field crops. In 1974, most of the farm was deeded to the province of BC for public parkland, campsites and trails. Now known as Ruckle Provincial Park, that land is bordered by 4 mi (7 km) of pristine shoreline. In 1990, Mike and Marjorie Lane began managing the farm on behalf of the Ruckle family, and they preserve the pioneer family's legacy by continuing to operate it as a working farm. The farm is known for producing organically raised Salt Spring lamb. Each year, the farm raises up to 150 lambs, along with highland beef, turkey, hens and pheasants. The large heritage orchard has apples, pears, cherries and plums, while the market garden yields a range of lettuce blends, peas, beans, squashes, tomatoes and corn—all available seasonally at the farm stand at the end of the driveway. The farm's organic meat is sold entirely on Salt Spring Island, to Hastings House Country House Hotel and through local grocery store Country Grocer.

NANOOSE EDIBLES ORGANIC FARM

Just north of Nanaimo in Nanoose Bay lies Nanoose Edibles Organic Farm, a sprawling, pastoral property that grows a bounty of BC-certified organic produce. Established in 1990 by husband and wife team Lorne and Barbara Ebell, the farm specializes in lettuces, arugula, and mustard and salad greens, along with a variety of vegetables, berries, orchard fruit and organic eggs. Firmly planted in the community, the farm hosts seasonal events and runs a weekly veggie box program for local residents. Visitors to the farm are invited to stroll the property, peruse the market stand and pick their own produce.

Rhubarb, Strawberry and Hazelnut Squares

MAKES 24 LARGE SQUARES

We know that spring has arrived when we bring bright, ruby red stalks of rhubarb into the kitchen and turn them into this sweet-tart dessert. The oatmeal base is firm for ease of handling—keeping crumbs on deck to a minimum. Select a variety of rhubarb stalks with deep red skins to add to the visual appeal. We like to pick up our rhubarb from the farm stand at Nanoose Edibles Organic Farm.

RHUBARB-STRAWBERRY FILLING

4 cups (1 L) coarsely chopped rhubarb

2 cups (475 mL) coarsely chopped strawberries

¾ cup (180 mL) granulated sugar

2½ Tbsp (37 mL) all-purpose flour

1 tsp (5 mL) cinnamon

OATMEAL BASE AND TOPPING

1¼ cups (300 mL) all-purpose flour

1 tsp (5 mL) baking soda

¼ tsp (1 mL) salt

¾ tsp (3.5 mL) cinnamon

2 cups (475 mL) quick-cooking oats

¾ cup (180 mL) packed brown sugar

1 cup (250 mL) unsalted butter, cut into small pieces

¾ cup (180 mL) roughly chopped hazelnuts

RHUBARB-STRAWBERRY FILLING Preheat oven to 375F (190C). In a large bowl, combine rhubarb and strawberries. Sprinkle with sugar, flour and cinnamon, and toss to combine. Spread mixture in a shallow roast pan. Roast for 10 minutes or until fruit has released just enough juice to blend with the sugar mixture but the pieces of fruit still retain their shape. Remove from oven, leaving oven on for finishing the squares.

OATMEAL BASE AND TOPPING In the bowl of an electric mixer, combine flour, baking soda, salt and cinnamon. Add oats and brown sugar. Mix. Add butter and mix at medium speed until just combined.

Line a 9- by 13-in (23- by 33-cm) baking pan with parchment paper. Lightly press 3 cups (710 mL) of the oatmeal mixture into the bottom of the pan. Cover base with rhubarb-strawberry filling.

Add hazelnuts to the remaining oatmeal mixture and sprinkle overtop. Bake until golden, approximately 30 minutes. Allow to cool in pan.

Gently lift uncut bars out of the pan by gripping the parchment paper. Transfer to a cutting board and cut into bars. Store in an airtight container.

Near the entrance to Von Donop Inlet,
Cortes Island, a group of boaters raft
up and enjoy each other's company.
JULIE BEAUREGARD-STEWART PHOTO

CHAPTER FIVE

ENTERTAINING
ON THE DOCK AND RAFTING UP

Meeting friends at the end of an exciting day of summer cruising gives everyone a chance to exchange their boating experiences. Sharing fine food and wine with family and friends might be done right at the dock, or it could mean tying up alongside each other while you are out on the water. Dips and appetizers are always popular at happy hour. Later, you might turn on the barbecue, prepare a large composed salad or throw together a simple pasta dish. The recipes in this section have been chosen with ease of entertaining in mind.

Tuna Tapenade

MAKES 1½ CUPS (350 ML)

This wonderful, Mediterranean-inspired spread can easily be made using pantry staples. When friends raft up for appetizers, duck below deck and whip some up to serve on crostini; a bunch of crunchy radishes with butter and sea salt flakes—a classic French combination—rounds out the platter. We like to use a Canadian albacore tuna processed at St. Jean's Cannery in Nanaimo. Leftovers are great for sandwiches the next day, especially if you have access to fresh artisanal bread.

⅓ cup (80 mL) mascarpone cheese

3 Tbsp (45 mL) extra-virgin olive oil, plus more for crostini

1 Tbsp (15 mL) Dijon Mustard

1 tsp (5 mL) lemon zest

Juice of ½ lemon

1 tsp (5 mL) anchovy paste

1 clove garlic, finely minced

3 Tbsp (45 mL) finely chopped flat-leaf parsley

½ cup (125 mL) pitted and finely chopped black olives

1 Tbsp (15 mL) chopped capers

1 tsp (5 mL) pepper

1 × 5.3 oz (150 gr) can solid albacore tuna, drained

¼ tsp (1 mL) salt

1 baguette, sliced into 1-in (2.5-cm) rounds

Radishes (optional)

Butter (optional)

Sea salt flakes (optional)

In a medium bowl, combine mascarpone cheese, olive oil, mustard, lemon zest, lemon juice, anchovy paste and garlic. Fold in parsley, black olives, capers and pepper. Using a fork, break tuna into chunks and tip it into the mascarpone mixture. Combine gently to retain the tuna's chunky texture. At this point, taste the tapenade to check for seasoning. Because some olives and capers are saltier than others, the amount of additional salt required will vary. If additional salt is needed, add a pinch. Set aside to allow flavours to marry while the bread is toasting.

Brush the tops of the baguette rounds with olive oil. Toast until golden under the broiler or on the barbecue, about 2 to 3 minutes each side.

Serve tapenade with crostini (and radishes, butter and sea salt flakes, if you wish).

Barbecued Brie with Thyme-Infused Honey

MAKES 1 MEDIUM-SIZED WHEEL OF BRIE

We love baking brie and wanted an option that didn't require turning on the oven. We experimented with grilling it on the barbecue and were pleasantly surprised at the outcome. While the brie does require careful supervision to ensure that it doesn't get too hot, this method is well worth the effort for the beautiful grill marks it imparts. We love using brie from Hilary's Cheese, located in Cowichan Bay, and serving it with a drizzling of honey from Yellow Point–based Fredrich's Honey that has been infused with thyme leaves.

⅓ cup (80 mL) liquid honey

A few sprigs thyme

1 medium-sized wheel of brie

1 loaf artisanal bread

In a small saucepan over medium heat, simmer honey and thyme sprigs together for 10 minutes.

Preheat barbecue to medium heat. Place brie on the barbecue and grill until soft, approximately 3 minutes per side.

Drizzle honey over brie and serve with bread.

FREDRICH'S HONEY

For the Fredrichs, crafting honey has been a family enterprise for over six decades. Theo Fredrich Sr., who first learned the art of honey-making as an apprentice in Germany, started Fredrich's Honey with his wife, Margaret, in 1966. Located in Yellow Point, just south of Nanaimo, the business is now run by Theo Fredrich Jr.—who grew up immersed in the family business—and his wife, Taylor. In addition to clear and creamed honey, the family produces pollen, bee bread and propolis. Fredrich's Honey products are sold at Thrifty Foods and 49th Parallel grocery stores.

Balsamic Beets and Goat's Cheese Crostini

MAKES 12 PIECES

When beets are roasted, their natural sweetness is heightened and concentrated. In this recipe, their flavour is balanced by the sharp tang of goat's cheese. We use the beautiful chèvres from the Salt Spring Island Cheese Company. The pairing is served on crostini to create a hearty, hand-held appetizer. To reduce your on-board preparation time, we suggest cooking the beets at home in advance.

6–8 small beets (purple and/or yellow), greens on

2 Tbsp (30 mL) olive oil, plus more for crostini

1 baguette, sliced into 12 pieces diagonally

1 clove garlic, minced

2 tsp (10 mL) balsamic vinegar

Pinch of granulated sugar

Salt and pepper

8 oz (226 gr) goat's cheese

Juice of ½ lemon

Preheat oven to 375F (190C). Trim beet greens 1 in (2.5 cm) above the top of the beets. Reserve beet greens and stems. Place beets in roasting pan, drizzle with 1 Tbsp (15 mL) olive oil and cover with aluminum foil. Roast until cooked through, approximately 30 minutes (or longer if needed). Beets are done when tender to the touch and a knife is inserted and removed without resistance. Remove from oven and allow to cool slightly so that they can be handled. While beets are still warm, rub off outer skin, then slice the beets into rounds. Set aside.

Brush tops of baguette pieces with olive oil. Toast under the broiler or on the barbecue until golden, 2 to 3 minutes a side. Wash and quarter beet greens and stems. Heat remaining 1 Tbsp (15 mL) olive oil in a non-stick sauté pan. Add garlic and cook until fragrant, approximately 30 seconds. Add stems, greens, balsamic vinegar and sugar. Season with salt and pepper. Cook until greens begin to wilt, approximately 2 minutes. Remove from heat.

In a bowl, combine goat's cheese with lemon juice, and add salt and pepper to taste.

Spread goat's cheese on crostini. Top with slices of roasted beets and beet greens and serve.

Crab Dip with Lemon, Capers and Dill

MAKES 2 CUPS (475 ML)

Dungeness crab is plentiful in our waters. Whether you catch them or purchase them, they need to be cleaned and cooked before you start this recipe. Then there is the time-consuming chore of removing the succulent meat from the shell. Having spent a considerable amount of time working with the crab so far, you certainly don't want to mask its delicate flavour with too many additions. Our crab dip is light, with a hint of lemon, capers and dill. Spoon it onto slices of fresh baguette and enjoy the fruits of your labour.

2 Tbsp (30 mL) mayonnaise

2 Tbsp (30 mL) plain Greek-style yogurt

Zest and juice of ½ lemon

1 tsp (5 mL) capers, finely chopped

3 tsp (15 mL) finely chopped fresh dill

Pinch of salt

2 cups (475 mL) cooked crabmeat

1 fresh baguette, sliced into 1-in (2.5-cm) rounds

Place all ingredients except crabmeat and bread in a bowl and mix well. Add crabmeat and stir in gently. Transfer dip to a serving bowl and serve with slices of fresh baguette.

Fresh herbs are the finishing touch on sweet and savoury dishes.

Nectarines, Prosciutto and Basil

MAKES 12 PIECES

Sweet, juicy nectarines from BC's fertile Okanagan Valley come into season during the summer months and are widely available on the coast. Wrapped in prosciutto with a basil leaf, they make for a simple appetizer that demonstrates how a few high-quality ingredients are all you need. Choose nectarines that aren't too firm.

3 ripe nectarines, pitted and quartered

6 long strips prosciutto, sliced in half lengthwise

12 large basil leaves

Wrap a piece of prosciutto around a piece of nectarine and a basil leaf. Serve at room temperature.

Sour Cherry Pâté

MAKES ONE 6-IN (15-CM) ROUND

This sweet, compact pâté made from dried cherries is a boater-friendly alternative to having pieces of dried fruit on your cheese tray. It pairs beautifully with everything from Salt Spring Island Cheese Company's chèvres (below) to a pungent blue from Hilary's Cheese (page 44). It can be thinly sliced on an as-needed basis and then wrapped up and stored in the galley for future use. Just right in a grilled cheese sandwich (page 161), or with dark chocolate and port-style wine for dessert, it is also lovely on its own if you have a sweet tooth.

¾ cup (180 mL) walnuts

2 cups (475 mL) dried sour cherries

1 Tbsp (15 mL) cherry brandy (kirsch)

1 tsp (5 mL) clear liquid honey

½ tsp (2.5 mL) allspice

Over medium heat, toast walnuts in a sauté pan for approximately 4 minutes, shaking the pan frequently. Set aside to cool. Once cool, finely chop walnuts in the bowl of a food processor and then tip them onto a plate. Set aside.

Place dried cherries, brandy, honey and allspice in a food processor and purée into a smooth paste.

On a clean surface, shape the cherry mixture into a disc approximately 6 in (15 cm) in diameter. Generously coat the disc with walnuts, pressing down to help them adhere on all sides. Wrap the disc loosely in parchment paper and store on the counter for a few days until it is dry enough to slice. Store in a cool spot in the galley.

Serve the pâté as an appetizer with local cheeses, fresh fruit, bread and crackers.

SALT SPRING ISLAND CHEESE COMPANY

Set on an idyllic, wooded farm, Salt Spring Island Cheese Company has been crafting handmade goat's and sheep's milk cheeses since 1994. Known primarily for their chèvres—which are artfully adorned with everything from basil and white truffles to lemon and edible flowers—owners David and Nancy Wood also produce feta, aged and surface-ripened cheeses. Visitors are invited to wander the property and greet the resident goats and sheep, watch the cheese-making process and sample all of the cheeses in the farm shop. On Salt Spring Island, the cheeses are available from the Village Market in Ganges Harbour, Thrifty Foods, Admiral's Specialty Foods and Patterson's General Store. They are also more widely available at Whole Foods Market and Thrifty Foods.

White Bean Hummus

MAKES 2 CUPS (475 ML)

When it's your turn to host happy hour, turn to your pantry and whip up this flavourful spread. A hand-held immersion blender will make for speedy preparation and a smooth consistency, however a potato masher is an excellent substitute and will just yield a chunkier consistency. Serve with crackers, toasted pita bread or Crisp Rosemary Flatbread (page 136).

⅓ cup (80 mL) olive oil

4 cloves garlic, diced

1 × 19 fl oz (540 mL) can white kidney beans, drained and rinsed

2 Tbsp (30 mL) freshly squeezed lemon juice

¾ tsp (3.5 mL) ground cumin

2 Tbsp (30 mL) chopped flat-leaf parsley

½ tsp (2.5 mL) salt

¾ tsp (3.5 mL) pepper

Heat olive oil in a small pan and add garlic. Cook until fragrant, about 30 seconds. Remove from heat and allow to cool. Combine all ingredients in a deep bowl and blend with an immersion blender until creamy. Store in an airtight container in the refrigerator. Serve at room temperature.

Crisp Rosemary Flatbread

MAKES FOUR FLATBREADS

The evening barbecue is a beloved ritual for cruisers, who relish cooking summer staples—grilled meats and roasted vegetables—outdoors. A fun way of using the barbecue is to grill flatbreads before dinner; our favourite recipe is this crisp version. Present these with cheeses, spreads and dips to your cruising companions and they will want to join you regularly. For ease of preparation on board, measure the dry ingredients into a zippered plastic bag at home in advance. Sage is an excellent substitute for the rosemary, if you want to try something different.

1¾ cups (415 mL) self-rising flour

2 Tbsp (30 mL) chopped fresh rosemary

½ tsp (2.5 mL) salt

½ cup (125 mL) warm water

⅓ cup (80 mL) olive oil

Several sprigs rosemary

Coarse sea salt

Preheat the barbecue on high heat. Mix first three ingredients in a bowl, leaving a well in the centre. Add water and olive oil and stir until a dough forms. Knead four or five times. Divide dough into four and roll out individually on parchment paper or pat by hand into thin discs.

Working on two discs at a time, brush with olive oil and top with rosemary sprigs, pressing them into the dough. Sprinkle with coarse sea salt. Transfer to the grill and cook for 2 minutes or until lightly browned. Turn and brown other side. Repeat the process for the two remaining discs. Serve while the flatbreads are still warm.

Dukkah

MAKES 1½ CUPS (350 ML)

We fell in love with dukkah, a mix of coarsely ground nuts, seeds and spices that is rooted in Egyptian cuisine, on a recent trip to New Zealand, where it is commonly served in winery tasting rooms. Our version uses local hazelnuts as the base ingredient, but other versions use almonds, pine nuts or macadamia nuts, use pumpkin seeds instead of sesame seeds, and use thyme instead of mint. Try our recipe and then experiment on your own. This appetizer is quick to prepare and easy to share—ideal when rafting up with friends after a day's outing. Make the dukkah at home and keep it stored in an airtight container in your galley pantry. To serve, have guests dip chunks of crusty bread in good olive oil and then into the aromatic mixture. Add a glass of wine and you are ready to share your adventures.

¾ cup (180 mL) hazelnuts

⅓ cup (80 mL) sesame seeds

2 Tbsp (30 mL) coriander seeds

2 Tbsp (30 mL) cumin seeds

1 tsp (5 mL) sea salt flakes

2 tsp (10 mL) pepper

1 Tbsp (15 mL) dried mint

Over medium heat, toast hazelnuts lightly in a shallow sauté pan for approximately 4 minutes, shaking the pan frequently. Place the nuts in a clean kitchen towel and rub to remove the loose skins. Transfer hazelnuts to the bowl of a food processor. Grind to a coarse consistency.

In the same pan, toast sesame seeds for 2 to 3 minutes. Add to hazelnuts. Toast coriander and cumin seeds for 2 minutes and add to the mixture in the bowl of the food processor. Add salt, pepper and mint and pulse until just combined. (Do not let it get to a powder consistency.) Store in an airtight container.

Serve with good-quality extra-virgin olive oil and fresh artisanal bread or baguette slices.

Albacore Tuna Niçoise with Anchovy Vinaigrette

SERVES FOUR

This hearty salad is a meal in itself—perfect for when you're feeding a group. While Niçoise salad often includes canned tuna, we love to use hot-smoked albacore tuna loin. The fish are line caught by the BC tuna fleet in the waters off the west coast of Vancouver Island; once on board, they are flash frozen at sea, to be processed once the boats return to harbour.

8 small new potatoes, cut in half

2 tsp (10 mL) salt

1 handful green beans

1 handful yellow beans

3–4 eggs

1 large bunch cherry tomatoes on the vine

Olive oil

Salt and pepper

1 cup (250 mL) black olives (preferably Niçoise)

1 lb (454 gr) hot-smoked albacore tuna loin, torn into serving-sized pieces

1 Tbsp (15 mL) torn flat-leaf parsley

4 cups (1 L) frisée salad greens, lightly packed

ANCHOVY VINAIGRETTE

2 anchovies (or 1½ tsp/7.5 mL anchovy paste)

2 tsp (10 mL) Dijon mustard

2 Tbsp (30 mL) red wine vinegar

1 small shallot, minced

1 clove garlic, minced

¼ cup (60 mL) plus 1 Tbsp (15 mL) olive oil

Pinch of granulated sugar

Salt and pepper

Preheat oven to 400F (205C). In a large pot of cold water, bring potatoes to a boil. Add 2 tsp (10 mL) salt and cook potatoes until tender, approximately 8 minutes. Drain. In a separate pot, blanch green and yellow beans in boiling water for 3 minutes, then drain and shock them in ice water so they maintain their bright colour.

Place eggs in a pot of cold water, bring to a boil and then remove the pan from the heat, cover with a lid and allow eggs to sit for 10 to 12 minutes. When the shells start to crack, the whites will be cooked through and the yolks will still be slightly soft. Peel the eggs and cut them in half.

Set cherry tomatoes on a baking sheet. Drizzle with olive oil and season with salt and pepper. Roast until skins begin to wrinkle, approximately 10 minutes.

ANCHOVY VINAIGRETTE In a small bowl, use the back of a fork to mash anchovies into a paste. Add mustard, vinegar, shallots and garlic. In a slow stream, whisk in olive oil until emulsified. Add sugar and season to taste with salt and pepper.

TO ASSEMBLE On a large serving platter, arrange potatoes, beans, tomatoes, olives and tuna. Top with eggs and garnish with parsley. Serve family-style with frisée and anchovy vinaigrette.

Grilled Flank Steak

SERVES SIX TO EIGHT

Flank steak is very useful to have in your freezer on extended cruises. A large one will feed a small group, and you'll likely have some left over—perfect for the next day's sandwiches or salad. Serve this steak with Grilled Root Vegetables (page 144) and Grilled Corn on the Cob with Compound Butters (page 143).

2 lbs (908 gr) flank steak

MARINADE
3 cloves garlic, minced
1 tsp (5 mL) Dijon mustard
½ tsp (2.5 mL) black pepper
¼ cup (60 mL) olive oil
¼ cup (60 mL) dry white wine
2 Tbsp (30 mL) white wine vinegar
2 Tbsp (30 mL) soy sauce

Combine all marinade ingredients in a large zippered plastic bag. Add steak and coat in marinade. Refrigerate for 3 hours, turning occasionally. Remove steak from the bag. Discard marinade.

Preheat barbecue to high heat. Cook steak to your preferred degree of doneness (7 minutes a side for medium). Remove from grill and cover with foil for 10 minutes. Slice thinly against the grain and serve.

Hot-Smoked Salmon and Boursin Cream with Pasta Shells

SERVES FOUR

In the northern islands, entertaining on board can be spontaneous, so it's important to have ingredients available that can be quickly made into an impressive dinner. In this dish, hot-smoked salmon punctuates a beautifully creamy sauce made with Boursin cheese, while crispy panko bread crumbs add crunch and texture. Ready in minutes, this dish gives you plenty of time to visit with your guests.

12 oz (340 gr) medium pasta shells

5.3 oz (150 gr) package Boursin cheese (or other soft herbed cheese)

1 cup (250 mL) whole milk

1 cup (250 mL) whipping cream

Zest of 1 lemon

Juice of ½ lemon

⅓ cup (80 mL) chopped mixed herbs (we use flat-leaf parsley, dill and chives)

1 cup (250 mL) panko bread crumbs

2 Tbsp (30 mL) olive oil

12 oz (340 gr) hot-smoked salmon, broken into bite-sized pieces

In a large pot, cook pasta in salted boiling water until al dente, approximately 10 minutes. Drain, reserving ½ cup (125 mL) of the cooking water.

Meanwhile, in a saucepan over medium heat, melt Boursin cheese. Add milk and cream and heat through. Add lemon zest and juice, along with the herbs.

Toast panko bread crumbs in olive oil in a sauté pan over medium-high heat until golden, approximately 5 minutes.

Combine the pasta and the cheese mixture. Stir in the reserved cooking water. Fold in salmon and top with toasted panko bread crumbs.

Grilled Corn on the Cob with Compound Butters

SERVES FOUR TO SIX

When Labour Day weekend arrives, fresh local corn is at its peak. The days are still warm and the barbecue is the preferred method of cooking for many boaters. Corn on the cob is a perfect side for anything that comes off your grill.

4–6 cobs of corn

GARLIC AND CHIVE BUTTER
1 clove garlic, minced
1 Tbsp (15 mL) minced chives
2 Tbsp (30 mL) butter, softened

LIME BUTTER
1 Tbsp (15 mL) lime zest
2 Tbsp (30 mL) butter, softened

SMOKED PAPRIKA BUTTER
Pinch of smoked paprika
2 Tbsp (30 mL) butter, softened

Preheat barbecue to high heat. Husk corn and place each cob on a piece of foil large enough to wrap it up in. Add 1 Tbsp (15 mL) water before sealing. Turn frequently on the grill until tender, approximately 10 minutes. Remove cobs from the foil and set them directly on the grill. Turn frequently for about 5 minutes to caramelize the kernels. Serve with one or more of the following compound butters.

BUTTER   For each compound butter recipe, simply combine the ingredients.

Grilled Root Vegetables

SERVES TWO

Because root vegetables take longer to cook than most summer vegetables, we speed up the process by cooking them in a sealed foil packet on the barbecue. If you are serving them with grilled steaks, pork chops or chicken, the cooking time will be approximately the same for both the meat and the vegetables. Other veggies that work well in these packets are sweet potatoes, parsnips, celery root and, of course, potatoes. Our recipe for Grilled Summer Vegetables is on page 97.

½ fennel bulb, sliced (half the fronds reserved and chopped)

1 medium carrot, peeled and cut into ½-in (1.3-cm) pieces

1 cup (250 mL) peeled and cubed butternut squash

1 yellow beet, peeled and cubed

1 sprig thyme, leaves removed

1 Tbsp (15 mL) finely chopped fresh rosemary

¼ tsp (1 mL) salt

Pinch of pepper

1 Tbsp (15 mL) butter, melted

1 Tbsp (15 mL) canola oil

Preheat barbecue to high heat. Toss all ingredients together in a bowl. Mound vegetables onto one side of a large piece of heavy foil and fold the other side over. Roll up edges to seal. Place packet on the barbecue and cook for approximately 15 minutes, turning frequently for even cooking.

To serve, top with fennel fronds.

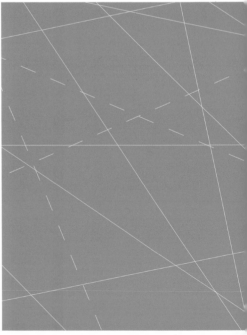

Roasted Stone Fruit with Mascarpone Cream

SERVES FOUR

Apricots, nectarines, peaches and plums from Okanagan Valley orchards are plentiful and widely available on the coast in the summer. Wonderful fresh and eaten out of the hand, they make a sweet addition to a meal prepared on the grill. The grilling process enhances and concentrates their natural sweetness. On a warm summer evening, enjoy this dessert in the cockpit while taking in the sunset with a glass of BC ice wine in hand.

2 Tbsp (30 mL) butter, melted

¼ cup (60 mL) roughly chopped hazelnuts

4 pieces stone fruit (we use apricots, peaches and nectarines)

2 Tbsp (30 mL) maple syrup (or liquid honey)

¼ cup (60 mL) Mascarpone Cream (page 230)

¾ cup (180 mL) roughly broken gingersnap cookies

Melt butter in a small pan on medium heat. Add hazelnuts, stirring frequently until they are slightly browned, approximately 4 minutes. Set aside to cool.

Slice stone fruit, removing stones. Arrange slices in a mound on a piece of heavy foil. Drizzle with maple syrup. Cover with foil and seal edges well to hold in juices. Set the fruit bundle on the grill at medium-high heat. Roast for approximately 5 minutes, then turn fruit over and grill for an additional 5 minutes or until the juices are bubbling. Remove from the grill and separate the fruit from the juices, pouring the juices into a small bowl.

Add mascarpone cream to the fruit juices and stir until well blended.

Divide fruit into four serving dishes. Pour mascarpone mixture over fruit. Top with broken gingersnap cookies and hazelnuts.

Cheesecake Nanaimo Bars

MAKES 16 LARGE SQUARES OR 25 SMALL SQUARES

Nanaimo, which we call home, is synonymous with its namesake chocolate-custard bars. They are said to have been created by coal miners' wives, who would send the desserts underground with their husbands. In this recipe, we've replaced the traditional sweet custard with a creamy cheesecake filling. The instant coffee added to the base heightens the chocolate flavour.

1½ cups (350 mL) chocolate cookie crumbs

½ cup (125 mL) unsweetened shredded coconut

½ cup (125 mL) hazelnuts, finely chopped

¾ cup (180 mL) unsalted butter, melted

2 tsp (10 mL) instant coffee powder

½ cup (125 mL) plus 2 Tbsp (30 mL) granulated sugar

1 lb (454 gr) cream cheese, at room temperature

¼ cup (60 mL) packed brown sugar

1 tsp (5 mL) vanilla extract

2 large eggs

1 cup (250 mL) semisweet chocolate chips or chunks

½ cup (125 mL) whipping cream

Preheat oven to 350F (175C). Line the bottom of a 9-in (23-cm) square metal baking pan with parchment paper.

Combine cookie crumbs, coconut, hazelnuts, butter, coffee powder and ¼ cup (60 mL) granulated sugar. Pat the mixture very firmly into the lined pan. Bake crust for 10 to 12 minutes or until lightly browned. Leaving the oven on for the next step, allow crust to cool to room temperature.

In a large bowl, beat cream cheese, brown sugar and ¼ cup (60 mL) granulated sugar until smooth. Beat in vanilla and eggs. Spread filling evenly over crust. Bake bars until edges are slightly puffed, approximately 10 minutes. Allow pan to cool on a rack for 30 minutes. Chill for at least 2 hours.

For ganache topping, bring 1 in (2.5 cm) water to a simmer in a medium saucepan. Combine chocolate with cream and remaining 2 Tbsp (30 mL) granulated sugar in a medium heatproof bowl. Place bowl directly over hot water and turn off heat. Let rest for 5 minutes and whisk until smooth. Spread warm ganache over the bars. Chill for at least 30 minutes.

Lift uncut squares out of the pan using the parchment paper. Cut into 16 or 25 squares, dipping knife in warm water and wiping it between cuts. Store in the refrigerator. May be served chilled or at room temperature.

Windalay II at rest in the afternoon
sun off East Redonda Island.
JULIE BEAUREGARD–STEWART PHOTO

CHAPTER SIX

NORTH

Extended cruising often means leaving the well-serviced southern islands and heading north to Desolation Sound, the Discovery Islands and as far as the stunning Broughton Archipelago.

In more remote areas, we turn to ingredients with a longer shelf life.

Rainbow Carrot Salad with Feta and Mint

SERVES FOUR

Easily stored in the outer storage lockers, carrots fare well on extended cruises. We often use beautiful rainbow carrots that we pick up at our local farmers' market. The feta brings a salty bite, while the mint adds freshness.

1 Tbsp (15 mL) Dijon mustard

2 tsp (10 mL) Harissa Spice Blend (page 225)

¼ cup (60 mL) extra-virgin olive oil

Juice of ½ lemon

Pinch of granulated sugar

6 medium carrots

¼ cup (60 mL) mint leaves

½ cup (125 mL) crumbled feta cheese

Salt and pepper

In a serving bowl, whisk together Dijon mustard, harissa blend, olive oil, lemon juice and sugar.

Peel carrots and cut into matchsticks. Transfer to the serving bowl.

Stack mint leaves and roll them lengthwise into one tight roll. Cut mint in chiffonade by slicing the roll thinly. Unravel the strips and transfer to the serving bowl.

Add feta to the serving bowl and toss salad. Season to taste with salt and pepper. Toss again and serve.

Green Apple and Kohlrabi Salad

SERVES FOUR

Made with hardy kohlrabi and green apple, this crisp salad is an ideal choice when the supply of salad greens is diminished. It goes well with the evening barbecue and makes a refreshing accompaniment to a lunch wrap.

2 cups (475 mL) peeled and julienned kohlrabi (approximately 1 large bulb)

1 Granny Smith apple, cored and diced

Sunflower sprouts (optional)

YOGURT AND LIME DRESSING

½ cup (125 mL) plain Greek-style yogurt

2 Tbsp (30 mL) fresh lemon juice

1 Tbsp (15 mL) coarse-grained mustard

3 Tbsp (45 mL) finely chopped flat-leaf parsley

½ tsp (2.5 mL) granulated sugar

Salt and pepper

Milk or water (optional)

In a bowl, whisk together yogurt, lemon juice, mustard, parsley and sugar. Season to taste with salt and pepper. If dressing is too thick, thin with milk or water until desired consistency is achieved.

Toss in kohlrabi and apple. Garnish each serving with sunflower sprouts, if using.

Tangled Kale Rotini with Warm Bacon Vinaigrette

SERVES TWO TO FOUR

Hailed as a superfood for its nutritional properties, kale is the leafy green vegetable of choice for many boaters thanks to its hardy texture. Somewhat bitter in its raw state, kale benefits from being "massaged" with oil and allowed to rest before eating. Unlike more fragile leafy greens, leftovers fare well in the refrigerator and are still crisp the next day.

6 large kale leaves, stems and ribs removed

¼ cup (60 mL) plus 2 Tbsp (30 mL) extra-virgin olive oil

6 oz (170 gr) rotini

2 Tbsp (30 mL) pine nuts

2 Tbsp (30 mL) Bacon Jam (page 220)

2 Tbsp (30 mL) red wine vinegar

Salt and pepper

Stack kale leaves and roll them lengthwise into one tight roll. Cut kale in chiffonade by slicing roll thinly. Unravel strips and place in a large serving bowl. Add 2 Tbsp (30 mL) olive oil and toss by hand. Set aside for 15 minutes.

Bring a large pot of salted water to a boil. Cook pasta for 10 to 12 minutes or until al dente. Drain.

In a small pan over medium heat, toast pine nuts for 3 minutes. Remove nuts from the pan and set aside.

In the same pan, heat bacon jam. Whisk in remaining olive oil and red wine vinegar.

Add pasta to the kale in the serving bowl. Toss with warm bacon vinaigrette. Top with pine nuts and serve.

White Bean and Sausage Soup

SERVES FOUR TO SIX

Perfect for a cozy evening below deck while anchored in a quiet cove, this hearty soup is quick to prepare and has wonderful depth of flavour, thanks to the red wine. White kidney beans (sometimes called cannellini beans) may be substituted for the navy beans.

3 large mild Italian sausages, skins removed

1 onion, chopped

2 cloves garlic, minced

1 × 28 fl oz (796 mL) can diced tomatoes

2 × 14 fl oz (398 mL) cans navy beans

1 cup (250 mL) red wine

Pinch of red pepper flakes

1 bay leaf

Salt and pepper

2–3 Tbsp coarsely chopped flat-leaf parsley, for garnish

Break up sausage meat and cook in a medium saucepan over medium heat. When partially cooked, add onions and garlic and heat until sausage is cooked through and onions are translucent, approximately 8 to 10 minutes total. Add tomatoes, beans, red wine, pepper flakes, bay leaf and 1 cup (250 mL) water. Season with salt and pepper. Bring to a boil. Reduce heat and simmer for 15 minutes.

Ladle into serving bowls and garnish with parsley.

Potato and Fennel Soup

SERVES FOUR TO SIX

This is a true stick-to-your-ribs soup that will warm the soul on a soggy day.

1 tsp (5 mL) fennel seeds

2 Tbsp (30 mL) olive oil

1 small onion, diced

1 fennel bulb, coarsely chopped (fronds reserved and chopped)

1 russet potato, peeled and diced

4 cups (1 L) chicken stock

½ cup (125 mL) whipping cream

Salt and pepper

In a large pot over medium heat, toast fennel seeds until fragrant, approximately 30 seconds. Add olive oil, onions, fennel and potatoes, and cook, stirring occasionally, until softened, approximately 10 minutes. Add chicken stock and simmer, covered, for 25 minutes or until the potatoes are fully cooked and the fennel is tender.

Purée the soup with an immersion blender until smooth. Add cream and season to taste with salt and pepper. Thin with additional stock if required.

To serve, top with reserved fennel fronds.

LEFT: Potato and Fennel Soup.
RIGHT: Carrot, Maple and Ginger Soup

Carrot, Maple and Ginger Soup

SERVES FOUR TO SIX

The immersion blender really earns its place in your toolbox with this soup. Made with carrots and onions—galley staples for most cruising cooks—this soup has real appeal for boaters as it can be prepared on board in no time. The chopping and sautéing are well worth the effort for all of the rich flavour this soup yields.

1 medium onion, diced

2 cloves garlic, finely minced

4 cups (1 L) peeled and chopped carrots

2 Tbsp (30 mL) canola oil

2 Tbsp (30 mL) maple syrup

2 Tbsp (30 mL) freshly grated ginger

4 cups (1 L) vegetable stock

1 tsp (5 mL) salt

Pepper

Plain Greek-style yogurt

Flat-leaf parsley and/or chives

In a heavy pot, sauté onions, garlic and carrots in canola oil over medium heat until soft. Add maple syrup and ginger and continue to cook over low heat for 10 minutes longer. Add vegetable stock, salt and pepper to taste.

Cover and simmer for another 10 minutes until the vegetables are tender. Purée the soup with an immersion blender.

Garnish each serving with a dollop of Greek-style yogurt and fresh herbs.

Pumpkin and Coconut Soup

SERVES FOUR TO SIX

Quick and easy to prepare yet bursting with flavour, this Thai-inspired soup is so good it tastes as if it were made from scratch with fresh, cooked pumpkin. The recipe relies on pantry staples, so it is a great one to save for the end of your cruising adventure.

2 Tbsp (30 mL) canola oil

1 onion, finely chopped

2 cloves garlic, crushed

1 × 28 oz (796 mL) can puréed pumpkin

3 cups (710 mL) chicken stock

1 × 14 fl oz (398 mL) can coconut milk

½ tsp (2.5 mL) red pepper flakes

Zest and juice of ½ lime

1 Tbsp (15 mL) yellow Thai curry paste

1 Tbsp (15 mL) fish sauce (optional)

Salt and pepper

2–3 Tbsp roughly chopped cilantro, for garnish

Heat canola oil in a large pot and gently cook onions until softened, about 3 minutes. Add garlic and cook until fragrant, approximately 30 seconds. Add all other ingredients except the cilantro and simmer for 20 minutes. Purée the soup with an immersion blender. Season to taste with salt and pepper. Garnish individual servings with cilantro.

Grilled Cheese, Three Ways

EACH RECIPE MAKES ONE SANDWICH

Grilled cheese sandwiches are always a hit on board. By heating both sides of the sandwich in the pan at the same time and then bringing it together at the end, the bread toasts more evenly and the cheese melts faster. The combinations below are three of our favourite twists on the classic.

APPLE, SAGE AND CHEDDAR
Sage leaves

Dijon mustard

2 slices rye bread

Aged white cheddar cheese, sliced

Few slices Granny Smith apple

Pepper

BACON JAM, TOMATO AND HAVARTI
Bacon Jam (page 220)

2 slices sourdough bread

Havarti, cut into thin slices

Tomato, cut into thin slices

SOUR CHERRY PÂTÉ AND BRIE
2 slices French bread

Brie, cut into slices

Sour Cherry Pâté (page 132)

To start each sandwich, heat 1 tsp (5 mL) butter and 1 tsp (5 mL) canola oil in a non-stick sauté pan over medium-high heat until sizzling.

APPLE, SAGE AND CHEDDAR Crisp sage leaves in pan, 30 seconds on each side, before you start cooking the sandwich. Set aside.

Thinly spread mustard on one side of each bread slice. Place both slices of bread in the pan, mustard side up, and top each piece with sliced cheddar. On one side, add the apple slices, crisp sage leaves and a sprinkling of pepper. Once the cheese has started to melt and the underside of the bread is nicely toasted, bring both halves of sandwich together and continue cooking until cheese is completely melted.

BACON JAM, TOMATO AND HAVARTI Spread a thin layer of bacon jam on one side of each bread slice. Place both slices of bread in the pan, bacon jam side up, and top one piece with sliced havarti. Once the cheese has started to melt and the underside of the bread is nicely toasted, top the cheesy piece of bread with sliced tomato and the other slice of bread. Continue cooking until the cheese is completely melted.

SOUR CHERRY PÂTÉ AND BRIE Place both slices of bread in the pan. Place sliced brie and thin slices of sour cherry pâté on one piece of bread. Once the cheese has started to melt and the underside of the bread is nicely toasted, top with the other slice of bread. Continue cooking until the cheese is completely melted.

Pantry Spaghettini

SERVES TWO

A well-provisioned pantry makes this simple pasta dish a recipe you'll fall back on time and time again. Just knowing you have the necessary ingredients in your arsenal helps make for a more stress-free holiday for the galley cook. This rings true for the home cook, as well. We made this spaghettini after unpacking from a boating trip when the refrigerator at home was bare. Full of flavour and taking only minutes to prepare, it fits the bill when time, provisions—and energy—are limited.

5 oz (141 gr) spaghettini

2 Tbsp (30 mL) olive oil

1 cup (250 mL) panko (or regular) bread crumbs

2 Tbsp (30 mL) Bacon Jam (page 220)

¼ cup (60 mL) sun-dried tomatoes in oil (or dried and rehydrated), drained and chopped

1 Tbsp (15 mL) capers

½ cup (125 mL) pitted and sliced black olives

Grated parmesan cheese

Bring a large pot of salted water to a boil. Add spaghettini to water and cook until al dente, about 6 to 8 minutes. Drain pasta, reserving 1 cup (250 mL) of the cooking water.

Meanwhile, heat 1 Tbsp (15 mL) olive oil in a large sauté pan. Add bread crumbs and cook until crisp and golden, approximately 5 minutes. Remove bread crumbs from the pan and set aside.

Add drained pasta to the pan along with reserved cooking water, bacon jam, sun-dried tomatoes, capers, olives and remaining 1 Tbsp (15 mL) olive oil. Toss to warm through. When ready to serve, toss through the bread crumbs. Serve with grated parmesan cheese.

Pearl Couscous Risotto

SERVES FOUR TO SIX

A relative newcomer—and welcome addition—to our galley pantry, pearl couscous (also known as Israeli couscous) makes a wonderful, creamy risotto that is ready in approximately 12 minutes. Larger than the traditional North African couscous, the pearl variety has a beautiful nutty flavour and can be substituted for rice in many recipes.

4 cups (1 L) chicken stock

1 cup (250 mL) pearl couscous

⅓ cup (80 mL) chopped flat-leaf parsley

Zest of 1 lemon

⅓ cup (80 mL) grated parmesan cheese

3 Tbsp (45 mL) butter

Salt and pepper

In a medium pot, bring chicken stock to a boil. Remove 2 cups (475 mL) of the hot stock from the pot and reserve. Add couscous to the 2 cups (475 mL) remaining in the pot. Reduce to a simmer and stir frequently for approximately 12 minutes or until cooked through. Add reserved stock ¼ cup (60 mL) at a time, as necessary, until the couscous is soft. (This process yields a creamy, risotto-like texture.) Fold in parsley, lemon zest, parmesan cheese and butter. Season to taste with salt and pepper, and serve.

Saffron-Scented Risotto with Chorizo and Clams

SERVES FOUR

When it's raining and you want to spend your time stirring slowly at the stove, risotto fits the bill. Inspired by paella, a Spanish rice dish brimming with a variety of meat, seafood and vegetables, this risotto showcases fresh Manila clams and spicy chorizo. Saffron, an integral ingredient in paella, is used here to create an aromatic broth.

3 cups (710 mL) chicken stock

Pinch of saffron

2 Tbsp (30 mL) canola oil

1 shallot, diced

2 fresh chorizo sausages, cut into bite-sized pieces

2 cloves garlic, minced

1 cup (250 mL) arborio rice

⅓ cup (80 mL) white wine

1 × 10 fl oz (284 mL) can clam nectar

1 Tbsp (15 mL) butter

¼ cup (60 mL) grated parmesan cheese

1½ lbs (681 gr) fresh Manila clams, in shells

¼ cup (60 mL) finely chopped flat-leaf parsley

In a medium pot, bring chicken stock and saffron to a simmer.

In a large pot over medium heat, heat canola oil and add shallots, chorizo and garlic. Sauté until vegetables are soft and chorizo is cooked through. Add rice to the pot and stir until the rice is fully coated and begins to brown, approximately 1 minute. Add white wine. Heat through. (The rice will begin to take on a shiny appearance.) Add clam nectar and heat through. Add stock, one ladleful at a time, until each is absorbed. Stir the rice well every time you add stock. Continue until the rice is nearly cooked and most of the stock has been used, approximately 20 minutes.

Add butter, parmesan cheese and clams. Stir well to combine and cover. Cook with the lid on until the clam shells open, approximately 5 minutes. Discard any clams that do not open. Mix in parsley before serving.

OPPOSITE PAGE, TOP LEFT: Lund, the jumping-off place for boaters on the way to Desolation Sound, features a quaint waterfront and the last chance for a restaurant meal.
ALISON MALONE EATHORNE PHOTO

Gnocchi with Butternut Squash, Fried Sage and Brown Butter

SERVES FOUR

A favourite homemade dish of ours is butternut squash ravioli with fried sage leaves and a beautiful brown butter. This boater-friendly version uses quick-cooking gnocchi—Italian potato dumplings—which can be purchased already vacuum packed. The hearty ingredients and savoury flavours make for a satisfying vegetarian dish.

6 Tbsp (90 mL) butter

1 clove garlic, finely chopped

4 cups (1 L) peeled and chopped butternut squash, cut into 1-in (2.5-cm) cubes

½ tsp (2.5 mL) salt

½ tsp (2.5 mL) pepper

2.2 lbs (1 kg) gnocchi

¼ cup (60 mL) sage leaves, roughly chopped

2 Tbsp (30 mL) cream

½ cup (125 mL) grated parmesan cheese, plus more for garnish

In a large sauté pan over medium heat, melt 2 Tbsp (30 mL) butter. Add garlic and cook for 1 minute. Add butternut squash, salt and pepper and toss to coat. Cook for 8 minutes or until the squash is tender, stirring frequently to prevent it from sticking. Remove the squash from the pan.

Meanwhile, bring a large pot of salted water to a boil. Add gnocchi and cook until they float to the surface, approximately 3 minutes. Drain.

Melt remaining 4 Tbsp (60 mL) butter in the pan over medium heat. Add sage and stir until it is crispy and butter begins to brown. (Watch carefully to ensure that it does not burn.) Add cream and heat through. Add gnocchi, squash and parmesan cheese, and toss. Heat through. To serve, garnish with additional parmesan cheese.

White Bean Gratin

SERVES TWO TO FOUR

This recipe found its way into our boating arsenal on the last night of an extended cruise when provisions were at their lowest. On a chilly evening, it makes a nice vegetarian main course or a side dish for roast chicken.

1 Tbsp (15 mL) olive oil

1 medium onion, finely chopped

1 tsp (5 mL) anchovy paste

2 cloves garlic, minced

2 × 19 fl oz (540 mL) cans white kidney beans, drained and rinsed

¼ cup (60 mL) vegetable stock

2 Tbsp (30 mL) coarsely chopped flat-leaf parsley

1 tsp (5 mL) finely chopped sage leaves

½ cup (125 mL) grated parmesan cheese

Salt and pepper

GRATIN TOPPING

1 cup (250 mL) bread crumbs

¼ cup (60 mL) grated parmesan cheese

1 clove garlic, minced

3 Tbsp (45 mL) melted butter

Preheat oven to 350F (175C). Heat olive oil in a medium skillet. Add onions and cook until translucent, approximately 5 minutes. Add anchovy paste and the 2 minced cloves garlic in the last 30 seconds. Add beans, vegetable stock, parsley and sage. Using the back of a spoon, mash half of the beans. Add parmesan cheese and season with salt and pepper. Spread evenly in an ovenproof dish.

In a bowl, make the gratin topping by combining the bread crumbs with parmesan cheese, garlic and melted butter. Sprinkle over the bean mixture.

Bake until the beans are bubbling and the bread crumb topping is golden, approximately 15 to 20 minutes, and serve.

Chicken Paillards with Lemon Butter

SERVES TWO

Thin, boneless cuts of meat called paillards (or escalopes) are ideal for the galley stove. Butterflied chicken breasts, thin slices of pork tenderloin and beef tenderloin steaks can be vacuum packed and stored in the freezer, then cooked in less than 10 minutes for a quick dinner. The key to this dish is the flavourful, creamy sauce that is made in the same pan by deglazing the poultry drippings with stock or wine. After letting the sauce cool slightly, lay the paillard on a serving plate and drizzle the pan-dripping sauce overtop. Top with a handful of lightly dressed arugula or other mixed greens when available. For a more substantial dish, serve the paillards over noodles, rice, mashed potatoes or quinoa.

2 boneless, skinless chicken breasts

Salt and pepper

1 Tbsp (15 mL) olive oil

1 Tbsp (15 mL) butter

Juice of ½ lemon

½ cup (125 mL) chicken stock (or white wine)

1–2 Tbsp chopped chives

Lay chicken breasts flat on a clean surface, use a sharp knife to slice most of the way through and open butterfly style. Season with salt and pepper on both sides. Heat olive oil and butter in a large skillet on medium-high heat until the pan begins to sizzle. Add breasts to the pan and cook for 2 to 3 minutes. Turn breasts over and cook on the other side for another 2 minutes. Remove chicken from the pan.

Add lemon juice and chicken stock to the pan. Using a spoon, scrape poultry drippings from the pan and stir them into the sauce. Simmer over low heat to reduce sauce until it coats a spoon, adding butter as needed for a richer flavour. Return chicken to the pan and coat with sauce. Garnish each serving with chives.

Pork Paillards with Creamy Mushroom Sauce

SERVES TWO

Thick Greek-style yogurt creates a velvety sauce, perfectly punctuated with smoked paprika.

4 thin slices pork tenderloin, each about 3 oz (85 gr) and ½ in (1.3 cm) thick

Salt and pepper

1 Tbsp (15 mL) canola oil

2 Tbsp (30 mL) butter

1 medium onion, thinly sliced

1 cup (250 mL) quartered fresh mushrooms (canned mushrooms may be substituted)

½ cup (125 mL) white wine

½ cup (125 mL) chicken stock

½ cup (125 mL) plain, high-fat, Greek-style yogurt (or sour cream)

½ tsp (2.5 mL) smoked paprika

Season pork slices with salt and pepper then brush both sides with canola oil. Heat pan to medium-high heat. Brown pork on one side for 2 minutes. Turn and cook through on the other side for approximately 2 minutes. Remove pork from the pan.

Melt butter in the pan and cook onions until translucent, approximately 5 minutes. Add mushrooms and cook until brown. Add white wine and chicken stock to the pan, stirring to loosen drippings from the bottom. Simmer sauce over medium-low heat until it reduces by half. Stir in yogurt and paprika. Return pork to the sauce, heat through and serve.

Beef Tenderloin Paillards with Mushroom and Red Wine Sauce

SERVES TWO

Red wine deglazes the pan to yield a deeply flavourful sauce.

2 Tbsp (30 mL) olive oil

1 small onion, sliced

1 clove garlic, minced

1 cup (250 mL) thickly sliced brown mushrooms

2 × 6–8 oz (170–226 gr) beef tenderloin steaks, cut to ½ in (1.3 cm) thickness

Salt and pepper

1 tsp (5 mL) Dijon mustard

¾ cup (180 mL) dry red wine

1 Tbsp (15 mL) butter

In heavy sauté pan, heat 1 Tbsp (15 mL) of the olive oil over medium-high heat. Sauté onions and garlic until softened, approximately 3 minutes. Add mushrooms and cook through, stirring frequently, approximately 6 minutes. Transfer to a bowl and cover.

Rub steaks with remaining olive oil. Sprinkle with salt and pepper. Brown over medium-high heat, approximately 4 minutes per side. Transfer to a warm plate. Cover and let rest for 5 minutes.

Add mustard and red wine to pan. Cook, scraping up brown bits, until reduced by half, approximately 3 minutes.

Add mushrooms and butter and continue to cook until the sauce has thickened, about 3 to 4 minutes. Serve sauce over the steaks.

Artisan Sausage with Bean Medley

SERVES FOUR

In this dish, our take on traditional pork and beans, we love to use artisanal garlic sausage from Ravenstone Farm Charcuterie, located in Qualicum Beach. The ale in the sauce gives this recipe great depth of flavour.

1½ lbs (680 gr) garlic sausage coil

1 medium onion, chopped

2 cloves garlic, minced

½ cup (125 mL) packed brown sugar

2 Tbsp (30 mL) tomato paste

1 tsp (5 mL) ground cumin

¼ tsp (1 mL) cayenne

½ cup (125 mL) ale, or more if needed

1 tsp (5 mL) salt

1 × 14 fl oz (398 mL) can diced tomatoes

1 × 19 fl oz (540 mL) can red kidney beans, drained but not rinsed

1 × 19 fl oz (540 mL) can white kidney beans, drained but not rinsed

1 × 14 fl oz (398 mL) can pinto beans, drained but not rinsed

Salt and pepper

 In a deep-sided sauté pan over medium heat, cook sausage coil for 8 minutes on each side. Remove from pan and cover with foil. Drain oil from pan, reserving 2 Tbsp (30 mL) in the pan.

Add onions and garlic to the pan and sauté until tender, approximately 3 minutes. Stir in brown sugar, tomato paste, cumin, cayenne, ale and salt. Simmer, uncovered, for 10 minutes or until onions are soft and translucent. Add canned tomatoes and beans. Cover and simmer on low heat for 20 minutes, stirring occasionally.

As the sauce thickens, add more ale as desired. Season to taste with salt and pepper. Set sausage coil atop the beans. Replace the lid and heat until the sausage has warmed through, approximately 5 minutes. To serve, cut the sausage coil into large pieces and serve with the beans.

RAVENSTONE FARM CHARCUTERIE

Since establishing Ravenstone Farm Charcuterie in 2010, owner Grant Smith has been delighting Vancouver Islanders with his all-natural pork, lamb and chicken products. Along with business partner Trevor Hooper, Smith raises purebred Clun Forest and Navajo Churro sheep, as well as Large Black, Berkshire and Landrace hogs on his 21-acre (8.5-ha) Qualicum Beach farm. Raised ethically and sustainably, the livestock are grass fed, pasture raised and free of antibiotics and hormones. Smith and Hooper produce a wide range of filler- and chemical-free artisan sausages (including chorizo, cognac and British banger varieties), along with whiskey-smoked bacon, ham and pulled pork. Ravenstone Farm also produces a variety of pork and lamb cuts, as well as whole roasting chickens, all prepared on site in their certified butcher shop. Ravenstone Farm Charcuterie's products are sold at mid-island farmers' markets and at Bread and Honey in Parksville.

Pan-Seared Duck with Lentils

SERVES FOUR

Inspired by the classic French pairing, this dish is rich, succulent and wonderful on a cool rainy evening—comfort food at its best. It has the texture and depth of flavour of a long-simmering stew but will, in fact, be ready in fewer than 30 minutes. (The cooking time is even shorter if you use canned lentils instead of dry.)

1 cup (250 mL) dry green or brown lentils, washed (or 4 × 14 fl oz/398 mL cans prepared lentils, drained and rinsed)

3 cups (710 mL) water

Salt and pepper

2 Tbsp (30 mL) canola oil

2 cloves garlic, minced

2 medium carrots, finely chopped

2 celery stalks, finely chopped

½ medium onion, finely chopped

4 × 6–8 oz (170–226 gr) duck breasts, boneless but skin on

1 cup (250 mL) chicken stock, plus up to ½ cup (125 mL) more as needed

½ cup (125 mL) white wine

¼ cup (60 mL) finely chopped flat-leaf parsley

In a medium saucepan, combine dry lentils with water and a pinch of salt. Bring to a boil, then reduce heat and simmer for 20 minutes or until lentils are just tender. Drain lentils, return to the saucepan and remove from heat.

In a deep-sided sauté pan, heat canola oil over medium heat. Add garlic, carrots, celery and onions. Sauté until vegetables are just tender, approximately 4 minutes. Stir carrot mixture into the lentils.

Score skin and underlying fat of duck breasts diagonally with cuts 1 in (2.5 cm) apart. Do not cut into meat. Season with salt and pepper. In the sauté pan, sear duck breasts, skin side down, over high heat. Cook for approximately 2 minutes and drain off fat. Cook for an additional 2 minutes and drain fat again. Skin should be crisp and brown. Turn duck breasts so that they are skin side up and cook for 6 minutes or until brown and the internal temperature reaches 145F (63C). Remove duck from the pan and tent with foil.

Return the sauté pan to the heat. Add chicken stock and white wine, scraping up drippings from the bottom of the pan. Bring to a boil and reduce heat to simmer. Return lentil mixture to the pan and heat through. If necessary, add more stock to achieve a sauce-like consistency. Stir in parsley and season to taste with salt and pepper.

Thinly slice the duck breasts and serve over the lentils.

Grilled Pork Loin with Apricot Chutney

SERVES TWO

Pork loin is an excellent cut of meat to take along on the boat. Lean and compact, it travels well in the freezer, takes only minutes to cook and can be used in a variety of dishes. We like to glaze it with apricot chutney and serve it over couscous. Leftovers piled on a crusty baguette make for a delicious lunch the next day.

1 lb (454 gr) pork loin
Olive oil
Salt and pepper

APRICOT CHUTNEY
3 cups (710 mL) roughly chopped apricots
⅓ cup (80 mL) packed light brown sugar
½ cup (125 mL) chopped Vidalia onions
¼ cup (60 mL) apple cider vinegar
¼ cup (60 mL) dried currants
2 Tbsp (30 mL) liquid honey
½ tsp (2.5 mL) salt
¼ tsp (1 mL) ground coriander
¼ tsp (1 mL) pepper

COUSCOUS
1 cup (250 mL) couscous
1¼ cup (300 mL) chicken stock

APRICOT CHUTNEY Combine all of the chutney ingredients in a saucepan over medium-high heat. Bring to a boil, then reduce heat and simmer until apricots and onions are cooked through, 10 to 12 minutes.

COUSCOUS Measure couscous into a bowl. Bring the chicken stock to a boil. Pour over couscous. Cover the bowl and leave for 5 minutes until couscous is softened and stock is absorbed.

GRILLED PORK Preheat barbecue to medium-low. (Because pork loin is very lean, grilling should be done over medium to low heat.) Oil grill to help prevent pork from sticking.

Lightly coat pork loin in olive oil. Season all sides with salt and pepper. Place pork on barbecue and grill, turning frequently, for approximately 15 minutes. Brush with apricot chutney and cook for an additional 5 minutes until the meat is cooked through and the chutney has formed a glaze. Serve over couscous with additional chutney on the side.

Apple and Vanilla Crisp

SERVES SIX TO EIGHT

Hands down, apple crisp has been served in our family home more often than any other dessert. For many years, Grandpa Hawken (Lorna's father) grew over 50 varieties of apples in his hobby orchard, as a result of his grafting expertise. Starting every July, he would deliver baskets of hand-picked apples that we, in turn, would happily consume. Apple crisp became the standby that any one of us could make, often without a recipe. The time-consuming part has always been the baking. We have found that this can be cut in half by starting the cooking process with the apples in a pan on top of the stove. Your galley will be redolent with the smells of apple pie.

6 cups (1.4 L) peeled and roughly chopped apples, preferably a mix of Braeburn and tart Granny Smith (approximately 6–7 medium apples)

¼ cup (60 mL) granulated sugar

1 vanilla bean, cut down the centre and seeds scraped out with the tip of a knife (or 1 tsp/ 5 mL vanilla extract)

Juice of ½ lemon

1 Tbsp (15 mL) all-purpose flour

TOPPING

½ cup (125 mL) all-purpose flour

½ cup (125 mL) rolled oats (not instant)

½ cup (125 mL) packed light brown sugar

1 tsp (5 mL) cinnamon

⅓ cup (80 mL) butter, at room temperature

½ cup (125 mL) hazelnuts, coarsely chopped

TO SERVE

Milk or cream, to pour over the crisp (optional)

Preheat oven to 375F (190C). Combine apples with sugar, vanilla bean seeds and lemon juice. In a large pan over medium heat, sauté apples for 5 to 7 minutes, until sugar is dissolved and apples are partially cooked. Remove from heat. Sift flour over apples and stir through.

For the topping, mix flour, oats, brown sugar and cinnamon together in a medium bowl. Add butter and combine until the mixture has a crumbly texture. Stir in hazelnuts. Pour apples and their liquid into a 9-in (23-cm) square baking pan. Sprinkle the topping over the apples.

Bake in the centre of the oven for 20 minutes, until the crisp is golden and the apples are fully cooked. If the pan is quite full, place a baking sheet on the rack below to catch drips.

May be served either warm or at room temperature, and with milk or cream poured overtop if desired.

Panforte

MAKES 16 WEDGES

It was while doing our Christmas baking years ago that a recipe for Italian panforte came to light. We tried it, loved it and realized that it was ideal for our catalogue of boating recipes. Prepared at home and stored in a sealed container, panforte can sit on the galley shelf without refrigeration. Here is our variation of the sweet treat that goes well with a mug of coffee when perched out on the rail.

1 cup (250 mL) whole almonds

1 cup (250 mL) whole hazelnuts

3 cups (710 mL) dried fruit (we use raisins, cranberries, apricots, figs and candied ginger)

¾ cup (180 mL) all-purpose flour

¼ cup (60 mL) cocoa powder, plus more for dusting

1 tsp (5 mL) cinnamon

½ tsp (2.5 mL) ground ginger

½ cup (125 mL) granulated sugar

¾ cup (180 mL) liquid honey

Toast almonds and hazelnuts in separate pans at 375F (190C) for 5 to 10 minutes or until lightly browned. Remove from oven and let cool. Wrap hazelnuts in a clean kitchen towel and rub to remove skins. Combine fruit and nuts in a bowl. Stir through flour, cocoa, cinnamon and ginger.

Heat sugar and honey in a heavy pot and boil until the mixture reaches the "soft ball" stage at 240F (115C). Pour the sugar syrup over the fruit mixture and stir until combined. Cool slightly until it can be handled (it is quite sticky), then press evenly into a lightly greased springform pan. Bake in a 300F (150C) oven for 35 minutes or until set. Remove from oven and allow to cool a little.

While slightly warm, remove the panforte from the pan and transfer to a cooling rack. Let cool completely, then dust with cocoa powder. Wrap the panforte in parchment paper. Store at room temperature in an airtight container. To serve, slice into narrow wedges.

Early morning fog rolls through the anchorage at Wyatt Bay, Quadra Island.

CHAPTER SEVEN

RACING

Sailors rounding the mark off Neah Bay or turning the corner around Cape Scott expect to encounter cold winds, rain and rough water. Such conditions demand meals that are quick to prepare and easy to eat when the crew is needed on the rail.

In addition to one-pot meals—which can be made ahead of time—consider meal-sized muffins and snack food that can be managed with cold hands. Because these days will not be easy on the cook, plan for simple-to-make and quick-to-clean-up meals that will keep you available for the next spinnaker change.

FEEDING A CREW

In the weeks leading up to each Van Isle 360 race, our dining room table looked like a military command station thanks to all the spreadsheets, lists and navigation charts. With all of our sails, spinnakers and gear on board, there was no way we could store a two-week supply of food and beverages for that many people, so we enlisted friends and family members to drive to ports of call such as Telegraph Cove, Port Hardy and Winter Harbour to meet us with our provisions for the remaining legs of the journey. Our land crew played an invaluable role in keeping the boat crew well fed.

Bacon, Leek and Cheddar Muffins

MAKES 12 EXTRA-LARGE MUFFINS

In the wee hours of the morning on the race course, nothing goes over better with the crew than a savoury muffin and a strong cup of coffee. Prior to our first Van Isle 360 race, I was overly ambitious with my baking, bringing along far more muffins than our crew could possibly consume. As we made our way to the start line of one of the legs, we found ourselves throwing extras to another boat that was short on provisions. These muffins—flaky, buttery and punctuated with the flavours of bacon, leek and aged cheddar—have been a boating staple ever since.

1 lb (454 gr) bacon, finely chopped

2 leeks, halved, washed, dried and finely chopped

3½ cups (830 mL) all-purpose flour

1 Tbsp (15 mL) plus 1 tsp (5 mL) baking powder

1 tsp (5 mL) baking soda

1 tsp (5 mL) salt

3 cups (710 mL) grated aged cheddar cheese

1 cup (250 mL) milk

½ cup (125 mL) plus 2 Tbsp (30 mL) canola oil

1 cup (250 mL) plain Greek-style yogurt

3 eggs

1 tsp (5 mL) pepper

Preheat oven to 400F (205C). Lightly grease muffin tins.

In a medium sauté pan over medium heat, cook bacon until crisp, approximately 10 minutes. Remove from pan and drain on paper towels. Add leeks to the pan of bacon grease and cook until soft, approximately 6 to 8 minutes. Drain and allow to cool with the bacon.

In a large bowl, sift together flour, baking powder, baking soda and salt. Stir in bacon, leeks and 2½ cups (600 mL) of the cheese.

In another large bowl, whisk milk, canola oil, yogurt, eggs and pepper together. Add the dry mixture to the wet ingredients, mixing until just combined.

Spoon the batter into muffin tins. Sprinkle the remaining ½ cup (125 mL) cheese on top. Bake for 12 minutes or until a toothpick inserted into the centre of a muffin comes out clean. Let stand for 5 minutes in the pan before transferring to a wire rack to cool completely. Store muffins in an airtight container.

West Coast Trail Muffins

MAKES 12 EXTRA-LARGE MUFFINS

Trail mix—a mixture of nuts, grains and dried fruit—is commonly carried along as a high-energy snack food by hikers on Vancouver Island's rigorous West Coast Trail. We thought the trail's name was befitting for this large, dense breakfast muffin packed full of many of the same ingredients.

TOPPING

2 Tbsp (30 mL) unsalted butter, chilled

⅓ cup (80 mL) all-purpose flour

¼ cup (60 mL) packed brown sugar

½ cup (125 mL) rolled oats

¼ cup (60 mL) shelled pumpkin seeds

2 Tbsp (30 mL) shelled sunflower seeds

2 Tbsp (30 mL) whole flax seeds

1 tsp (5 mL) water

1 tsp (5 mL) canola oil

1½ Tbsp (22.5 mL) liquid honey

MUFFINS

1¾ cups (415 mL) all-purpose flour

2 tsp (10 mL) baking powder

2 tsp (10 mL) cinnamon

¼ tsp (1 mL) salt

4 eggs

⅓ cup (80 mL) canola oil

⅓ cup (80 mL) plain Greek-style yogurt

1 cup (250 mL) granulated sugar

2 tsp (10 mL) vanilla extract

1⅓ cups (330 mL) grated carrots

1 Granny Smith apple, cored and grated

¾ cup (180 mL) chopped walnuts

¾ cup (180 mL) dried cranberries

½ cup (125 mL) shredded coconut

TOPPING ↪ For the topping, use a fork to mix together butter, flour and brown sugar to a crumbly consistency. Stir in remaining ingredients and set aside.

MUFFINS ↪ Preheat oven to 350F (175C). Grease muffin tins.

Sift flour, baking powder, cinnamon and salt into a bowl.

In a large bowl, whisk together eggs, canola oil, yogurt, sugar and vanilla. Add carrots, apples, walnuts, cranberries and coconut. Gently fold in the flour mixture until most of the flour is moist. Do not overstir.

Spoon the batter into muffin tins. Sprinkle with the topping and bake for 25 minutes or until a toothpick inserted into the centre of a muffin comes out clean. Cool muffins in the pan for 5 minutes, then remove from the tins and cool completely on a rack.

Store muffins in an airtight container. When the sea conditions are demanding and cooking is no longer a priority, a stash of these muffins fills the breakfast order. ↩

Coastal Cluster Granola

MAKES 8 CUPS (2 L)

If you have been looking for a granola recipe that makes crunchy, nutty granola clusters, this is the one to try. We love to layer it with Blueberry, Lemon and Thyme Compote (page 223), thick Greek-style yogurt and fresh raspberries, although it's wonderful with any other fresh, stewed or roasted fruit. You may also find yourself reaching for a handful of this granola when you need a quick snack at any time of day.

3 cups (710 mL) whole rolled oats (not instant)

3 cups (710 mL) mixed nuts and seeds (we use walnuts, sunflower seeds and almonds)

1 tsp (5 mL) cinnamon

½ tsp (2.5 mL) ground cardamom

½ tsp (2.5 mL) nutmeg

½ cup (125 mL) unsalted butter

1 cup (250 mL) firmly packed brown sugar

⅓ cup (80 mL) water

½ tsp (2.5 mL) salt

2 tsp (10 mL) vanilla extract

1 cup (250 mL) mixed dried fruit (we use cranberries, blueberries and apricots)

Preheat oven to 300F (150C). Grease a baking sheet. In the bowl of a food processor, grind 1 cup (250 mL) of the oats to a fine powder. In a mixing bowl, combine ground oats with the remaining 2 cups (500 mL) of oats and the nuts and spices.

In a saucepan over medium-high heat, combine butter, brown sugar and water. Heat until the mixture begins to bubble. Remove from heat and stir in salt and vanilla. Pour this sugar syrup over the oats and nuts and combine well. Gently push the mixture into clusters on a baking sheet and cook for 30 minutes. Stir to break larger clusters and cook for an additional 10 minutes. Remove from oven. Let cool completely on the baking sheet. Add dry fruit and store in an airtight container.

Oatmeal with Maple-Cinnamon Apples and Toasted Walnuts

SERVES THREE TO FOUR

Cool mornings are generally the order of the day on the water in the Pacific Northwest. A bowl of oatmeal porridge that comes together in fewer than 10 minutes is a lovely way to kickstart the morning after your bare feet have hit the cold cabin sole. Thanks to its subtle nutty flavour, oatmeal is a good vehicle for a wide variety of fruits, nuts and spices. We love this version with its toasted walnuts and slices of McIntosh apple cooked in maple syrup, cinnamon and rum. Oatmeal with peaches, along with Mascarpone Cream (page 230) that has been flavoured with honey and vanilla, is another go-to version—a twist on a childhood favourite. Experiment with stone fruit, berries, various nuts, nutmeg, allspice and cloves.

1¼ cups (300 mL) whole rolled oats (not instant)

3 cups (710 mL) water

Pinch of salt

1 McIntosh apple, peeled, cored and chopped

2 Tbsp (30 mL) maple syrup, plus more for when serving

½ tsp (2.5 mL) cinnamon

1 Tbsp (15 mL) dark rum (optional)

¼ cup (60 mL) chopped walnuts, toasted

¾–1 cup (180–250 mL) milk (about ¼ cup/60 mL per serving)

Over medium heat, mix oats with water and salt in a saucepan. Simmer 6 to 8 minutes, stirring frequently, until oats are soft.

In a small sauté pan over medium-high heat, simmer apple pieces in maple syrup, cinnamon and rum, if using, for 5 minutes or until tender.

To serve, top oatmeal with apples, walnuts, milk and additional syrup, if desired, in individual bowls.

CLOCKWISE FROM TOP: Crew members enjoy their view from the windward rail as their boat works to weather. DAVE HEATH PHOTO. *Aeriel* finds safe harbour after a day on the race course. DAVE HEATH PHOTO. Bill and Ryan are geared up for a night sail down the west coast of Vancouver Island. PAT MAHONEY PHOTO

Muffin-Tin Frittatas, Three Ways

SERVES SIX

A breakfast favourite for our crew of eight was always an egg and ham breakfast sandwich. In lumpy seas, I would scramble the eggs, warm the ham, melt cheese overtop and then assemble it all on English muffins, one at a time. It was always quite a production and I wish I discovered the muffin-tin method years ago. We now bake individual frittatas—filled with our favourite ingredients—in muffin tins in the oven and have them in English muffins. These sandwiches go over extremely well with a tired, hungry crew at the beginning of what is sure to be a long day on the course. If you wish to simplify the preparation process even further, cook the eggs before leaving the dock and keep them warm in the oven in a baking tray covered with foil. Once it's time to serve, tuck the frittatas into English muffins that have been warmed in the oven for a few minutes. A smearing of our Bacon Jam (page 220) and a thick slice of tomato are delicious additions, as well.

WITH SERRANO HAM

6 thin slices Serrano ham

6 eggs

6 slices aged cheddar cheese

6 English muffins

WITH SERRANO HAM Preheat oven to 350F (175C). Lightly grease a six-portion, standard-sized muffin tin. Loosely fold a slice of Serrano ham into each cup. Crack an egg into each cup. For a shorter cooking time, prick the yolks. Top each with a slice of cheese. Bake for 15 minutes for a well-done egg or until the yolk is set to your liking. During the last few minutes of baking, warm English muffins in the oven in a pan. Lift frittatas out of muffin cups using a spoon and serve in English muffins.

WITH SUN-DRIED TOMATOES AND GOAT'S CHEESE

6 eggs

¼ cup (60 mL) sun-dried tomatoes, drained and diced

¼ cup (60 mL) crumbled goat's cheese

2 Tbsp (30 mL) finely chopped fresh chives or flat-leaf parsley (optional)

6 English muffins

WITH SUN-DRIED TOMATOES AND GOAT'S CHEESE Preheat oven to 350F (175C). Lightly grease a six-portion, standard-sized muffin tin. Crack eggs into a bowl and beat well with a whisk. Mix in sun-dried tomatoes, goat's cheese and chives. Pour into six muffin cups. Bake for 15 minutes, until set. During the last few minutes of baking, warm English muffins in the oven in a pan. Lift frittatas out of muffin cups using a spoon and serve in English muffins.

. . . CONTINUED ON NEXT PAGE

WITH SMOKED SALMON AND GOAT'S CHEESE

6 eggs

¼ cup (60 mL) smoked salmon, broken into small pieces

¼ cup (60 mL) goat's cheese, crumbled

1 handful sprouts (such as pea shoots or sunflower sprouts), for garnish

6 English muffins

WITH SMOKED SALMON AND GOAT'S CHEESE Preheat oven to 350F (175C). Lightly grease a six-portion, standard-sized muffin tin. Crack eggs into a bowl and beat well with a whisk. Mix in smoked salmon and goat's cheese. Pour into six muffin cups. Bake for 15 minutes, until set. During the last few minutes of baking, warm English muffins in the oven in a pan. Lift frittatas out of muffin cups using a spoon and serve with sprouts in English muffins.

OPPOSITE PAGE: Bacon jam and sliced tomato are excellent additions to muffin-tin frittatas.

Sausage and Fennel Hand Pies

SERVES EIGHT

These hand pies—filled with the warm flavours of sausage, fennel and apple—make for a substantial meal on a morning when you know that the day's travels could be arduous and there might not be a lot of cooking until you cross the finish line late in the day. Baked and frozen at home, they can be warmed through, wrapped in parchment and then easily passed up to the cockpit. These hand pies are crisp and flaky too, so they are best eaten right over the rail.

1 lb (454 gr) mild Italian pork (or turkey) sausage, any casings removed

1 Tbsp (15 mL) canola oil

½ medium white onion, diced

½ fennel bulb, diced

½ cup (125 mL) apple juice

1 tsp (5 mL) fennel seeds

¼ tsp (1 mL) salt

¼ tsp (1 mL) pepper

1 Tbsp (15 mL) all-purpose flour

1 × 14 oz (397 gr) package frozen puff pastry, thawed

1 egg

1 Tbsp (15 mL) water

In a large pan over medium-high heat, break up sausage and cook just until there is no pink showing. Add canola oil, onions and fennel and sauté until the vegetables are partially cooked. Add apple juice, fennel seeds, salt and pepper. Bring to a boil, then reduce to a simmer and cook until the vegetables are tender and the liquid has been reduced by half, approximately 15 minutes. Remove from heat and sprinkle flour over the sausage and vegetables. Mix well.

Preheat oven to 400F (205C). Line two large baking sheets with parchment paper. Remove puff pastry from the refrigerator and let stand 5 to 10 minutes at room temperature. Dust counter with flour. Divide dough in half, working with one half at a time. With a rolling pin, roll pastry out thin into a 12-in (30-cm) square. Cut into four squares. Place 2 Tbsp (30 mL) or more of the meat and vegetable mixture into centre of each piece of pastry.

Make an egg wash by whisking together egg and water. Working on one hand pie at a time, brush the edges of the dough with egg wash. Fold one corner over to the opposite corner, creating a triangle. Seal the edges by pressing down along them with the tines of a fork. Brush the pie surface with egg wash. Transfer hand pies to a baking sheet. Repeat process with remaining puff pastry and filling. Chill in the refrigerator for 15 minutes prior to baking.

Bake the pies for approximately 25 minutes or until golden brown. Allow to cool slightly before serving. If serving at a later time, let the pies cool completely before wrapping up and refrigerating or freezing. Frozen pies may be reheated on a baking sheet in a 350F (175C) oven for 15 to 20 minutes or until warmed through.

Pulled Pork Sandwiches with Fennel and Apple Slaw ❀

SERVES EIGHT

Pulled pork sandwiches make an easy, satisfying meal whether you're feeding two or a crew. After warming it through, cut open a packet and empty the contents onto a large bun. Fennel and apple slaw piled atop the pork adds an excellent contrast of flavour and texture, while our barbecue sauce adds further sweetness and spice.

1 × 5–6 lb (2.3–2.7 kg) pork shoulder roast

BRINE SOLUTION

½ cup (125 mL) salt

½ cup (125 mL) packed brown sugar

2 bay leaves

3 Tbsp (45 mL) dry rub mix

6 cups (1.4 L) water

DRY RUB

1 Tbsp (15 mL) cayenne

1 Tbsp (15 mL) chili powder

1 Tbsp (15 mL) ground cumin

1 Tbsp (15 mL) garlic powder

1 Tbsp (15 mL) onion powder

1 Tbsp (15 mL) sweet paprika

½ cup (125 mL) packed brown sugar

BRINE SOLUTION ↷ Combine brine solution ingredients in large pot and stir well. Add pork shoulder. If necessary, add additional water to cover the pork completely. Refrigerate overnight.

Remove pork from the brine. Dry it with paper towels and then cover all surfaces with dry rub, reserving ¼ cup (60 mL) of the rub for the barbecue sauce (see below). Place pork, fat side up, in a pot with a tight-fitting lid. Roast in a 225F (107C) oven for 5 hours.

When pork pulls apart easily, remove from the pot. Reserve liquid. Let the roast cool, then remove excess fat. Pull pork into long threads and put the meat into a large bowl. If you'd like the pulled pork to be a bit juicier for your sandwiches, add some reserved liquid.

If the pulled pork is not going to be used right away, it should be vacuum packed in one- to two-serving pouches and frozen for future use.

DRY RUB ↷ Combine dry rub ingredients and set aside. ↶

SWEET AND SPICY BARBECUE SAUCE

2 cups (475 mL) ketchup

1 cup (250 mL) water

¼ cup (60 mL) liquid honey

¼ cup (60 mL) molasses

¼ cup (60 mL) dry rub (see above)

2 Tbsp (30 mL) apple cider vinegar

FENNEL AND APPLE SLAW

2 large fennel bulbs, thinly sliced (fronds reserved and chopped)

2 Granny Smith apples, thinly sliced

½ Vidalia onion, thinly sliced

½ cup (125 mL) chopped walnuts

DRESSING

½ cup (125 mL) canola oil

3 Tbsp (45 mL) white wine vinegar

1 Tbsp (15 mL) Dijon mustard

1 tsp (5 mL) liquid honey

Salt and pepper

TO SERVE

8 large ciabatta (or kaiser) buns

SWEET AND SPICY BARBECUE SAUCE Combine all ingredients in a pot. Bring to a boil, then reduce to a simmer. Cook for 20 minutes. Use right away or allow to cool and refrigerate or freeze in an airtight container.

FENNEL AND APPLE SLAW Combine fennel, apple and onion slices in a serving bowl. Mix in fennel fronds.

Toast walnuts in a pan over medium heat, shaking the pan frequently, until lightly browned, approximately 5 minutes. Let cool and add to the fennel and apple mixture. Measure all dressing ingredients into a container with a tight-fitting lid. Secure lid and shake until well blended. Pour the dressing over the salad and toss.

TO SERVE Pile a generous amount of pulled pork onto a bun. Top with barbecue sauce and fennel and apple slaw.

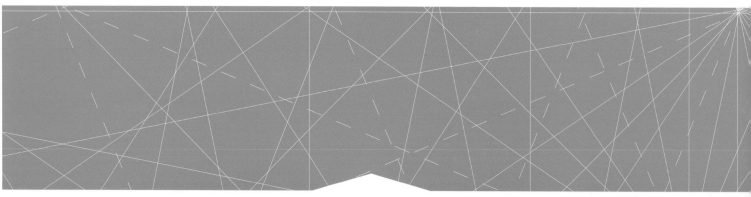

Chorizo and Lentil Soup ✸

SERVES SIX TO EIGHT

When the conditions are cold and wet for a racing crew sitting out on the rail, or the cruiser making passage, the question always asked is, "Are we having fun yet?" One might wonder how the response could ever be positive, but it is amazing what a big mug filled with warm, hearty soup can do for the spirits. This stick-to-your-ribs lentil soup—our updated take on split pea and ham—fits the bill. Not only is it delicious, but it always solicits a "Yes." To shorten the cooking time, substitute canned, prepared lentils for the dry lentils.

2 cups (475 mL) dry brown lentils, washed (or 6 × 14 fl oz/398 mL cans prepared lentils, drained and rinsed)

10 cups (2.4 L) chicken stock

2 bay leaves

1 large onion, finely chopped

1 carrot, peeled and finely chopped

2 Tbsp (30 mL) olive oil

¼ cup (60 mL) tomato paste

2 large cloves garlic, crushed

2 tsp (10 mL) smoked paprika

2 dried chorizo sausages, diced

2 × 14 fl oz (398 mL) cans diced tomatoes

Salt and pepper

¼ cup (60 mL) chopped cilantro

½ cup (125 mL) plain Greek-style yogurt

Combine lentils, chicken stock and bay leaves in a large pot. Bring the mixture to a boil, then reduce heat and simmer 30 minutes. In a non-stick pan over medium heat, sauté onions and carrots in olive oil until soft, approximately 5 minutes. Stir in tomato paste, garlic, paprika and diced chorizo, blending well. Add the chorizo and vegetable mixture to the lentils. Add tomatoes and season with salt and pepper. Bring to a boil, reduce heat and simmer, covered, for 20 to 30 minutes or until the lentils are tender, stirring occasionally.

If you are preparing the soup ahead of time, let cool and then vacuum pack in one- to two-person portions and freeze until use. Serve in individual bowls with a dollop of Greek-style yogurt.

Chicken, Chickpea and Butternut Squash Stew ✳

SERVES SIX

Packed with chicken, chickpeas and butternut squash, this hearty stew is classic comfort food—with a twist. Seasoned with a North African–inspired combination of warm spices, it is richly flavoured yet mild in heat. Serve with couscous, and your crew will think for a moment that they have sailed off to exotic climes.

4 cups (1 L) chicken stock

1 × 5½ fl oz (156 mL) can tomato paste

1½ tsp (7.5 mL) ground cumin

1 tsp (5 mL) salt

¼ tsp (1 mL) cayenne

Pinch of cinnamon

½ cup (125 mL) dried currants

1 medium onion, diced

3 cloves garlic, minced

5 cups (1.2 L) peeled, seeded and cubed butternut squash, in 1-in (2.5-cm) pieces (about 1 medium squash)

1 × 19 fl oz (540 mL) can chickpeas, drained and rinsed

2 lbs (908 gr) chicken thighs, skin and bones removed

1½ cups (350 mL) frozen peas

COUSCOUS

2 cups (475 mL) couscous

2½ cups (600 mL) chicken stock

GARNISH

½ cup (125 mL) slivered almonds (or pistachio nuts)

In a large pot, combine the 4 cups (1 L) chicken stock with tomato paste, cumin, salt, cayenne and cinnamon. Add currants, onions, garlic, squash, chickpeas and chicken. Bring to a gentle boil over medium-high heat. Reduce heat to low. Cover and simmer for 25 to 30 minutes or until the squash is tender and the chicken is cooked through. Add peas for the last 5 minutes of cooking time.

If you are preparing the stew ahead of time, let cool and then vacuum pack in one- to two-person portions and freeze until use.

COUSCOUS Measure couscous into a bowl. Bring the 2½ cups (600 mL) chicken stock to a boil. Pour over couscous. Cover the bowl and leave for 5 minutes until couscous is softened and stock is absorbed.

TO SERVE Serve stew over couscous in individual bowls. Garnish with slivered almonds.

Beef, Mushroom and Barley Soup

SERVES EIGHT

With several people and piles of gear on board, simple food is paramount on the race course. Throw in especially rough conditions and a boat on a heel, and the last thing you need is a three-ring circus in the galley. One-pot dishes answer the call. This rich soup has a thick, stew-like consistency thanks to the starch in the pearl barley.

2 lbs (908 gr) stewing beef, cut into bite-sized pieces

Salt and pepper

2 Tbsp (30 mL) olive oil

1 large onion, diced

1 cup (250 mL) pearl barley

1 cup (250 mL) red wine

12 cups (3 L) beef stock

3 carrots, peeled and diced

2 cups (475 mL) coarsely chopped mushrooms

2 Tbsp (30 mL) fresh thyme leaves

1 celery root, peeled and chopped

⅓ cup (80 mL) finely chopped flat-leaf parsley

Season beef with salt and pepper. In a large pot, heat olive oil and brown meat in batches until golden, approximately 5 minutes per batch. Add onions to the pot and continue cooking beef in batches until it is browned on all sides and onions are softened. Add barley, red wine and beef stock. Bring to a boil, then reduce heat and simmer for 30 minutes.

Add carrots, mushrooms and thyme and simmer for 10 minutes. Add celery root and simmer for an additional 15 minutes or until the vegetables are cooked through. Add parsley and season to taste with salt and pepper.

If you are preparing the soup ahead of time, allow to cool and then vacuum pack in one- to two-person portions and freeze until use. Serve in individual bowls.

Bison and Potato Pie ✸

SERVES SIX

Over the years, one of the dishes most requested by the racing crew has been shepherd's pie. In this version, we've used island-raised, grass-fed bison, which has a slightly sweeter flavour than beef. For ease of preparation on board, we've eliminated the long reheating time in the oven by simply warming the bison mixture in the vacuum-packed pouches and topping each portion with potato and goat's cheese mash. In foul weather, satisfying doesn't even begin to describe this dish.

2.2 lbs (1 kg) ground bison

6 slices bacon, diced

1 Tbsp (15 mL) butter

1 medium onion, diced

1 carrot, diced

1 stalk celery, diced

2 cloves garlic, minced

¼ cup (60 mL) all-purpose flour

¾ cup (180 mL) dry red wine

1 cup (250 mL) beef stock

1 × 14 fl oz (398 mL) can diced tomatoes

1 bay leaf

1 tsp (5 mL) fresh thyme leaves

½ tsp (2.5 mL) Worcestershire sauce

2 Tbsp (30 mL) coarsely chopped flat-leaf parsley

Salt and pepper

POTATO AND GOAT'S CHEESE MASH

4 russet potatoes, peeled and quartered

½ cup (125 mL) whole milk

3 Tbsp (45 mL) butter

4 oz (112 gr) goat's cheese

Salt and pepper

↩ In a large pot, cook bison over medium-high heat until browned, approximately 12 minutes. Add bacon, butter, onions, carrots and celery to the pot and sauté until bacon crisps and vegetables are soft, approximately 7 minutes. Add garlic and heat through until fragrant, about 30 seconds. Add flour to the pot and stir continuously until flour and fat combine, approximately 4 minutes. Add red wine, beef stock, tomatoes, bay leaf, thyme and Worcestershire sauce. Bring to a boil, then simmer, uncovered, for 15 minutes. Add parsley and season to taste with salt and pepper. Allow to cool. Vacuum pack in one- to two-person portions and freeze until use.

POTATO AND GOAT'S CHEESE MASH ↪ While bison mixture is reheating, bring potatoes to a boil in a large pot of cold, salted water. Reduce heat and simmer until a fork inserted comes out easily, approximately 14 minutes. Drain potatoes and mash using a hand-held masher. Mix in milk, butter and goat's cheese. Season to taste with salt and pepper.

TO SERVE ↪ Serve reheated bison mixture in individual bowls. Top with potato and goat's cheese mash. ↩

Five-Spice Beef with Noodles

SERVES EIGHT TO TEN

Simmered slowly in a fragrant Chinese five-spice blend of cinnamon, cloves, fennel seeds, Szechuan pepper-corns and star anise, this shredded beef is tender and aromatic. When you need a quick, comforting meal during rough conditions, simply add udon or other Asian noodles to the reheated beef and garnish with fresh vegetables. The beef also works well in other dishes, such as our Market Summer Roll (page 75). And the results are well worth the time and effort.

1 × 4 lb (1.8 kg) top-blade boneless roast, divided into 4 pieces for ease of cooking (or 4 thick-cut boneless blade steaks)

FIVE-SPICE STEAK RUB

2 tsp (10 mL) five-spice powder

1 Tbsp (15 mL) garlic powder

1 Tbsp (15 mL) ground ginger

¼ cup (60 mL) canola oil, plus more for browning

BRAISING LIQUID

1 large onion, sliced

4 cloves garlic, finely chopped

2 Tbsp (30 mL) finely chopped ginger

1 tsp (5 mL) red pepper flakes

2 Tbsp (30 mL) packed brown sugar

5 whole star anise

2 Tbsp (30 mL) black peppercorns

1 cinnamon stick

1 orange, cut in half

1 bunch cilantro

⅓ cup (80 mL) sake

¼ cup (60 mL) tamari

½ cup (125 mL) orange juice

1 cup (250 mL) red wine

3 cups (710 mL) beef stock

Combine spices and canola oil. Coat beef in the rub. Brown beef in a large ovenware pot over medium-high heat, using additional canola oil as needed. Remove beef from the pot and set aside. Reserve pot.

Preheat oven to 350F (175C). Using the same ovenware pot, sauté onions, garlic, ginger and pepper flakes, using additional canola oil if needed, until onions have softened, approximately 3 minutes. Add the rest of the braising liquid ingredients and bring to a boil. Remove from heat and return beef to the pot. Cover with a tight-fitting lid and braise in the oven for 1 hour and 45 minutes or until tender.

. . . CONTINUED ON NEXT PAGE

NOODLES AND GARNISH

12–16 oz (300–454 gr) instant udon noodles (or noodles of your choice)

Carrots, shredded, for garnish

Green onions, cut diagonally, for garnish

Other garnish such as sliced red chilies, cilantro or sesame seeds

Remove beef from the pot and strain the braising liquid into a bowl. Discard solids and reserve the liquid. Use two forks to shred the beef as you would shred pulled pork. Return shredded beef and strained sauce to the pot and stir to combine.

Allow beef to cool. Vacuum pack in one- to two-person portions and freeze until use.

When ready to serve, add udon noodles and heat through—or prepare your noodles separately if you are reheating the beef and then mix them together. Garnish with carrots and green onions, and/or other toppings such as red chilies, cilantro and sesame seeds.

Turkey and Quinoa Loaf with Potato Mash ✵

SERVES SIX TO EIGHT

In this recipe, we've lightened up traditional meatloaf with lean ground turkey and protein-packed quinoa. Cranberries, sage, thyme and orange zest hint at the flavours of traditional bread stuffing. Serve this loaf with mashed potatoes, and your crew will think they've sat down at the Thanksgiving dinner table. While we love to make gravy from scratch at home, we aren't averse to using a good-quality dried turkey or mushroom gravy mix on the boat—it would be a good addition to the meal.

TURKEY AND QUINOA LOAF

⅓ cup (80 mL) dried cranberries

1 small onion, finely chopped

2 cloves garlic, minced

2 stalks celery, finely chopped

1 Tbsp (15 mL) finely minced sage leaves

1 tsp (5 mL) fresh thyme leaves

1 Tbsp (15 mL) olive oil

2 lbs (908 gr) lean ground turkey

2 cups (500 mL) cooked quinoa

1 egg

¼ cup (60 mL) finely chopped flat-leaf parsley

Zest of ½ orange

1 tsp (5 mL) salt

1 tsp (5 mL) pepper

POTATO MASH

4 russet potatoes, peeled and quartered

½ cup (125 mL) whole milk

3 Tbsp (45 mL) butter

Salt and pepper

TURKEY AND QUINOA LOAF ↬ Reconstitute dried cranberries in a small bowl with warm water. Set aside for 15 minutes.

Preheat oven to 350F (175C). In a small pan, sauté onions, garlic, celery, sage and thyme in olive oil on medium heat for 5 to 7 minutes or until onions are translucent. Set aside to cool.

In a mixing bowl, combine turkey, quinoa, egg, parsley, orange zest, salt and pepper. Add cooled onion, garlic and celery mixture, and drained, reconstituted cranberries.

Transfer the mixture to a greased 9- by 5-in (23- by 13-cm) loaf pan and spread evenly. Cook 1¼ hours or until a thermometer inserted into the centre reads 170F (77C).

If vacuum packing the meatloaf, allow to cool and cut into six to eight servings. Vacuum pack in one- to two-person portions and freeze until use.

POTATO MASH ↬ While the loaf servings are reheating, bring potatoes to a boil in a large pot of salted water. Reduce heat and simmer until a fork comes out easily, about 14 minutes. Drain potatoes and mash using a hand-held masher. Mix in milk and butter. Season to taste with salt and pepper.

TO SERVE ↬ Serve the turkey and quinoa loaf on individual plates with potato mash. ↜

Sun-Dried Tomato Chicken

SERVES FOUR

When you need something really substantial on the course, this dish delivers in spades. During one of our Van Isle 360 experiences, the race was delayed due to stormy seas and we found ourselves with an extra night in Winter Harbour on the west coast of Vancouver Island. An extra batch of this dish, frozen in vacuum-packed pouches, saved the day when I needed to provide dinner for the crew.

2 tsp (10 mL) salt, plus more for seasoning

1 tsp (5 mL) pepper, plus more for seasoning

½ cup (125 mL) all-purpose flour

8 chicken thighs, skin and bones removed

3 Tbsp (45 mL) olive oil

1 onion, chopped

3 cloves garlic, finely chopped

1 large red pepper, chopped

¾ cup (180 mL) dry white wine

⅓ cup (80 mL) oil-packed sun-dried tomatoes, rinsed and coarsely chopped

1 × 28 fl oz (796 mL) can diced tomatoes

¾ cup (180 mL) chicken stock

1½ tsp (7.5 mL) dried oregano

1½ tsp (7.5 mL) dried basil

12 oz (340 gr) rotini (or other pasta)

In a small bowl, combine salt, pepper and flour. Coat chicken thighs in the flour mixture. In a large heavy pan, heat olive oil over medium-high heat. Working in batches if necessary, brown thighs in the pan, approximately 5 minutes per side. Remove chicken from pan and set aside.

Add onions, garlic and red peppers to the same pan and sauté over medium heat until the vegetables are softened, approximately 5 minutes. Season with salt and pepper. Add white wine, sun-dried tomatoes, canned tomatoes, chicken stock, oregano and basil. Bring sauce just to a boil and reduce heat to low. Return thighs to the pan and simmer until chicken is cooked through, approximately 25 minutes or until juices run clear.

If you are not serving it right away, allow chicken and sauce to cool. Vacuum pack in one- to two-person portions and freeze until use.

While the chicken is cooking (or reheating), bring a large pot of salted water to a boil. Cook pasta for 10 to 12 minutes or until al dente. Drain.

Serve the chicken and sauce over the rotini in individual bowls.

Double Chocolate Zucchini Bread

MAKES ONE LOAF

Sailing at night in the waters around Vancouver Island brings another element to the sport of sailboat racing. At four o'clock in the morning, "bone chilling" is often the best way to describe the conditions. It is cold, dark and quite possibly wet. A slice of this double chocolate zucchini bread, along with a hot chocolate or strong coffee, is just the pick-me-up to help see the crew through until daylight.

¾ cup (180 mL) granulated sugar

3 Tbsp (45 mL) canola oil

2 large eggs

½ cup (125 mL) plain Greek-style yogurt

½ cup (125 mL) applesauce

2 cups (475 mL) all-purpose flour

2 Tbsp (30 mL) unsweetened cocoa

1¼ tsp (6 mL) baking soda

½ tsp (2.5 mL) ground nutmeg

¼ tsp (1 mL) salt

1½ cups (350 mL) grated zucchini (approximately 2 small zucchini)

½ cup (125 mL) semisweet chocolate chips

½ cup (125 mL) chopped walnuts

Preheat oven to 350F (175C). Using a mixer, beat sugar, canola oil and eggs together in a large bowl until well blended. Stir in yogurt and applesauce.

In a separate bowl, combine flour, cocoa, baking soda, nutmeg and salt. Add dry mixture to wet mixture in two stages, blending just until moist. Stir in zucchini, chocolate chips and walnuts. Spoon batter into a lightly greased 9- by 5-in (23- by 13-cm) loaf pan.

Bake for 1 hour or until a toothpick inserted into the centre comes out clean. Cool loaf in the pan for 10 minutes, then remove from the pan. Cool completely on a wire rack. Wrap in plastic wrap and store at room temperature.

Chocolate Chip Cookies Spiked with Cinnamon, Cardamom and Chipotle

MAKES 24 COOKIES

This recipe takes our favourite chocolate chip cookie recipe to new heights thanks to subtle hits of cinnamon, cardamom and chipotle. Moist and dense, these cookies have satisfied many a sailor on rainy afternoons at sea.

3 cups (710 mL) all-purpose flour

1½ tsp (7.5 mL) baking soda

1½ tsp (7.5 mL) salt

2 tsp (10 mL) cinnamon

½ tsp (2.5 mL) ground cardamom

½ tsp (2.5 mL) chipotle chili powder

1 cup (250 mL) unsalted butter, melted and cooled

1½ cups (350 mL) packed light brown sugar

1 cup (250 mL) granulated sugar

3 large eggs

1½ tsp (7.5 mL) vanilla extract

2 cups (475 mL) semisweet chocolate chips

Position a rack in the middle of the oven and preheat to 375F (190C). Line two large baking sheets with parchment paper or non-stick baking mats.

Whisk together flour, baking soda, salt, cinnamon, cardamom and chipotle chili powder in a medium bowl. Set aside.

Beat together butter and both sugars in a large bowl with an electric mixer at high speed until pale and fluffy, 2 to 3 minutes. Beat in one egg at a time, mixing well in between, and beat until creamy. Beat in vanilla. Reduce speed to low and mix in flour mixture until just blended. Stir in chocolate chips.

Scoop ¼ cup (60 mL) of batter for each cookie, arranging mounds 3 in (7.6 cm) apart on two baking sheets. Flatten mounds into 3-in (7.6-cm) rounds using the palm of your hand (wet your hand first to prevent sticking).

Bake the cookies, one sheet at a time, until golden, 13 to 15 minutes. Transfer the cookies to a rack to cool. Store in an airtight container at room temperature.

Cranberry and Hazelnut Coffee Cake

MAKES 12 SLICES

Rich and moist (thanks to thick Greek-style yogurt), this delicious coffee cake is perfect with coffee during the late-afternoon slump. Topped with a few fresh berries, it makes a lovely dessert in the evening.

2 cups (475 mL) all-purpose flour

1 tsp (5 mL) baking powder

1 tsp (5 mL) baking soda

1 tsp (5 mL) salt

½ cup (125 mL) unsalted butter

1 cup (250 mL) granulated sugar

2 large eggs

1 tsp (5 mL) vanilla extract

1 cup (250 mL) plain Greek-style yogurt

CRANBERRY FILLING

1 cup (250 mL) fresh or frozen (thawed) cranberries

⅓ cup (80 mL) granulated sugar

¼ cup (60 mL) water

HAZELNUT TOPPING

1 cup (250 mL) all-purpose flour

⅓ cup (80 mL) packed light brown sugar

1 tsp (5 mL) cinnamon

½ tsp (2.5 mL) salt

½ cup (125 mL) butter, cut into small pieces

1 cup (250 mL) hazelnuts, roughly chopped

Preheat oven to 350F (175C). Grease a 9-in (23-cm) bundt or tube pan. In a small bowl, combine flour, baking powder, baking soda and salt. Using an electric mixer, combine butter, sugar, eggs and vanilla in a large bowl until smooth, approximately 3 minutes. Alternately fold flour mixture and yogurt into this wet mixture until just combined. Do not overmix.

Meanwhile, in a saucepan over medium-high heat, mix together cranberries, sugar and water. Bring to a boil, then reduce to a simmer and cook until the filling has a thick consistency, approximately 12 minutes. Remove from heat and let cool.

Spread half the batter in baking pan. Drizzle cranberry filling around the centre of the batter. Keep filling away from the sides of the pan to prevent burning. Top with remaining batter and smooth with a spatula.

For the topping, combine flour, brown sugar, cinnamon and salt. Work in the butter until it is in pea-sized pieces. Stir through the hazelnuts. Roughly distribute the topping over the cake. Bake for 40 minutes or until the cake springs back when touched.

Set the pan on a cooling rack. Transport the cake in the bundt pan or a large circular airtight container. The cake does not require refrigeration.

Trail Bars

MAKES 12 LARGE RECTANGULAR BARS OR 24 SQUARES

We conjured up the idea for these bars after years of passing bags of trail mix around the cockpit. By the end of the day, the boat would be littered with stray nuts, seeds and pieces of dried fruit. Packed full of nutritious ingredients—such as sunflower seeds, flax seeds and dried cranberries—these bars have a soft, chewy texture and do not require refrigeration. They are equally wonderful as a snack or as a quick breakfast item, and a great addition to the boater's inventory. Once you've tried these bars, we're confident that they'll become a family favourite both on and off the boat. We like to use locally grown and dried cranberries from farmers' markets and small shops around the island.

2½ cups (600 mL) quick-cooking rolled oats

⅓ cup (80 mL) ground almonds

⅓ cup (80 mL) chopped almonds

½ cup (125 mL) shelled sunflower seeds

½ cup (125 mL) sesame seeds

½ cup (125 mL) whole flax seeds

½ cup (125 mL) whole oats

⅓ cup (80 mL) dried cranberries

⅓ cup (80 mL) dried apples, chopped

½ cup (125 mL) butter

½ cup (125 mL) liquid honey

1 cup (250 mL) packed light brown sugar

Preheat oven to 300F (150C). Line a 9- by 13-in (23- by 33-cm) baking pan with parchment paper. Spray the paper lightly with cooking oil. Set aside.

In the bowl of a food processor, pulse 1 cup (250 mL) of the rolled oats to a flour-like consistency. Transfer to a large bowl and combine with the remaining 1½ cups (350 mL) rolled oats. Mix in all of the nuts, seeds, grains and dried fruit.

In a saucepan over medium heat, melt butter, honey and sugar together until the mixture is close to boiling. Pour the liquid over the dry ingredients and combine thoroughly. Spread this mixture in the baking pan and press down evenly. Bake for 30 minutes.

Let the uncut bars cool in the pan on a wire rack. Lift the bars from the pan to a cutting board using the parchment paper. Cut with a serrated knife by pressing down firmly onto the board. Store the bars in an airtight container at room temperature.

CHAPTER EIGHT
CONDIMENTS,
ETC.

In addition to the purchased condiments listed in our Toolbox section, we like to make a few of our own. While some of them are best made at home (denoted by the MA icon), most of them can easily be made on board. Aside from the Harissa Spice Blend and the Hazelnut Chocolate Spread, which are stored in your pantry, the condiments listed below will keep well in airtight containers in your refrigerator or icebox for the duration of your journey.

Arugula and Walnut Pesto

MAKES 1 CUP (250 ML)

While we'll always appreciate the classic basil and pine nut pesto, we love to experiment with other nuts and herbs, as well. This delicious arugula and walnut combination will keep in the refrigerator or icebox for up to five days.

⅓ cup (80 mL) walnuts

1 clove garlic

2 cups (475 mL) arugula, tightly packed

¼ cup (60 mL) grated parmesan cheese

Juice of ½ lemon

⅓ cup (80 mL) extra-virgin olive oil

In the bowl of a food processor, chop walnuts until fine. Add garlic, arugula, parmesan cheese and lemon juice. Purée. With the food processor on, add olive oil in a slow stream. Refrigerate in an airtight container until ready to use.

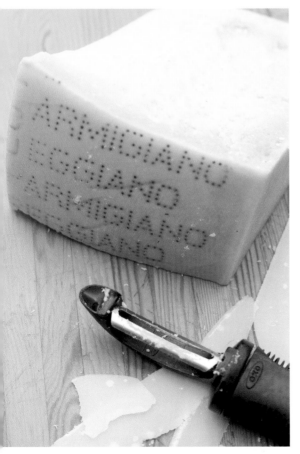

Bacon Jam

MAKES 1½ CUPS (350 ML)

A cornerstone of our toolbox, this make-ahead condiment imparts dishes with the smoky, sweet flavour of bacon—without creating a mess in the galley. For a hearty brunch, we smear it on toast and top it with a fried egg, aged cheddar, tomato and avocado. It adds depth of flavour to soups, stews and sauces, too.

1 lb (454 gr) bacon, cut into 1-in (2.5-cm) pieces

4 cloves garlic, chopped

1 medium onion, thinly sliced

3 Tbsp (45 mL) packed brown sugar

1 tsp (5 mL) Tabasco sauce, or to taste

1 cup (250 mL) brewed coffee

¼ cup (60 mL) apple cider vinegar

¼ cup (60 mL) maple syrup

½ tsp (2.5 mL) pepper

In a deep pan, fry bacon in batches until lightly browned and beginning to crisp. Remove bacon from the pan with a slotted spoon and set aside. Drain bacon fat from pan, leaving only about 2 Tbsp (30 mL).

Add garlic and onions to the rendered bacon fat and fry over medium heat for 5 minutes or until translucent. Return bacon to the pan and add all remaining ingredients. Simmer uncovered for 2 hours, adding ¼ cup (60 mL) water every 30 minutes. Consistency should be thick and jam-like.

Pulse bacon mixture in a food processor for 2 to 3 seconds, leaving some texture. Allow to cool. Keep refrigerated in an airtight container.

Plum and Vanilla Bean Compote

MAKES 2 CUPS (475 ML)

For decades, the plum tree in our backyard has provided us with an annual bounty of ripe fruit, which we have then turned into all manner of desserts and preserves. This simple recipe can be used for any ripe stone fruit you have on hand.

2 cups (475 mL) peeled and sliced ripe plums

½ cup (125 mL) granulated sugar

Juice of ½ lemon

1 vanilla bean, seeds removed with tip of a sharp knife

In a medium pot, combine plum slices, sugar, lemon juice and vanilla bean seeds. Simmer for 15 to 20 minutes until the mixture has reduced and is the consistency of syrup. Serve warm. Refrigerate in an airtight container.

Blueberry, Lemon and Thyme Compote

MAKES 2½ CUPS (600 ML)

A delicious compote will go a long way in your galley menu. For breakfast, serve fruit compote with granola and yogurt; for a simple dessert, it is lovely with Mascarpone Cream (page 230) and a slice of pound cake.

In this compote, the lemon zest and juice provide wonderful tartness, while the thyme imparts an unexpected earthiness.

⅓ cup (80 mL) water

¼ cup (60 mL) granulated sugar

Zest of 1 lemon

Small bunch thyme (tied with string), plus 1 tsp (5 mL) thyme leaves

3 cups (710 mL) blueberries

Juice of ½ lemon

In a medium saucepan over medium heat, simmer water, sugar, lemon zest and the bunch of thyme for 5 minutes. Turn off the heat and allow to steep for 5 minutes. Strain lemon zest and thyme from the liquid. Add 2 cups (475 mL) of the blueberries to the simple syrup you have just created. Cook for 10 minutes over medium heat, stirring often. Add the last 1 cup (250 mL) blueberries and cook for 5 minutes. Add the lemon juice and the 1 tsp (5 mL) thyme leaves. Allow to cool before serving. Refrigerate in an airtight container.

Habanero and Red Pepper Jelly

MAKES 3 CUPS (710 ML)

We have kicked up the heat in our favourite red pepper jelly by adding a habanero pepper. The added kick makes this jelly a great accompaniment for barbecued meat and the happy hour cheese tray. Adjust the amount of habanero according to your preferred level of heat—our version yields a medium heat. If you'd prefer a mild jelly, use just half a pepper.

4 red peppers

1 habanero pepper

½ cup (125 mL) apple cider vinegar

½ cup (125 mL) white wine vinegar

1½ cups (350 mL) granulated sugar

¼ tsp (1 mL) salt

Remove seeds from red peppers and habanero pepper and chop coarsely. Handle the habanero pepper with gloves or paper towels. Avoid contact with your bare hands or eyes. Place chopped peppers in a medium pot with cider vinegar and white wine vinegar. Bring to a boil, then reduce to a simmer. Cook until peppers are soft, approximately 15 minutes. Pour the mixture into the bowl of a food processor and purée until smooth.

Return pepper mixture to the pot. Add sugar and salt and gently stir over low heat until the sugar dissolves. Bring to a boil, then lower heat and simmer for an additional 20 to 25 minutes until partially thickened. Remove from heat. Allow the jelly to cool, then store it in an airtight container in your refrigerator or icebox.

Harissa Spice Blend and Paste

MAKES ¾ CUP (180 ML) SPICE BLEND

This North African spice blend is a handy item to have in the galley pantry. Highly seasoned, it is commonly found in paste form, blended with garlic cloves and tomato paste. Our boater-friendly dried version does not require refrigeration. When you're ready to use it, simply mix it with olive oil and lemon juice. Whether used dry or in paste form, it works well as a rub for barbecued meat and as a flavouring for couscous, soups, stews and salad dressings; blend the paste with mayonnaise to make a flavourful condiment for sandwiches, burgers and wraps. A little goes a long way. Adjust to your preferred level of heat by experimenting with the amount of cayenne.

2 Tbsp (30 mL) sun-dried tomatoes (dried, not packed in oil)

¼ cup (60 mL) sweet paprika

2 Tbsp (30 mL) cayenne

2 Tbsp (30 mL) ground cumin

1 Tbsp (15 mL) ground coriander

1 Tbsp (15 mL) garlic powder

2 tsp (10 mL) salt

PASTE

Olive oil

Lemon juice

Grind dried tomatoes to a powder in a spice grinder. In a bowl, combine ground tomatoes with the other dry ingredients. Store in an airtight container in your pantry.

When ready to use, add equal parts dry ingredients, olive oil and lemon juice to create a thick paste. Combine 1 tsp (5 mL) of each to make 1 Tbsp (15 mL) of paste. Prepare only what you require for your dish. Let the mixture rest for 30 minutes before using, to bring out the full flavour of the spices.

Hazelnut Chocolate Spread

MAKES 2 CUPS (475 ML)

Vancouver Island–grown hazelnuts are combined with cocoa to produce a thick, satisfying spread that can be used for breakfast (smeared on a thick slice of bread) or dessert (warmed and drizzled over sweet summer berries). We like to use hazelnuts from Foote's Hazelnut Farm in Chemainus.

2 cups (475 mL) hazelnuts

½ cup (125 mL) unsweetened cocoa powder

1 cup (250 mL) powdered sugar

½ tsp (2.5 mL) vanilla extract

¼ tsp (1 mL) salt

3½ Tbsp (52.5 mL) hazelnut oil, or more if needed

Preheat oven to 400F (205C). Spread hazelnuts evenly over a cookie sheet and toast until they have darkened and become aromatic, approximately 10 minutes. While the nuts are warm, transfer to a damp kitchen towel and rub to remove the skins.

In a food processor, grind hazelnuts to a very smooth butter, scraping the sides as needed, approximately 5 minutes. Add cocoa, sugar, vanilla, salt and hazelnut oil to the food processor and continue to process until well blended, approximately 2 minutes. The finished spread should have the consistency of peanut butter. If it is too dry, add extra hazelnut oil by the tablespoon. Store in an airtight container in your pantry.

FOOTE'S HAZELNUT FARM

A fiftieth birthday gift has grown into a flourishing hazelnut farm in Chemainus, located just north of Duncan. Valerie Foote purchased 25 hazelnut trees for her husband, Terry, in 1996; today, the couple operates a 900-tree orchard, producing pesticide-free shelled and in-shell nuts. Every October, the Footes harvest more than 10,000 pounds (4,500 kilograms) of nuts, which are sold out by December. The couple continues to expand their land and expects to increase their annual production by a third by 2014. The Footes' hazelnuts are available at Quality Foods, Nesvog Meats (Nanaimo), Cowichan Valley Meat Market (Duncan), Ladysmith Health Foods Store and directly from the farm.

Lemon and Dill Yogurt

MAKES ¾ CUP (180 ML)

This delicious yogurt dip will really earn its place in your refrigerator or icebox. Smear it on burgers, sandwiches and wraps, or use it as a dip for vegetables.

¾ cup (180 mL) plain Greek-style yogurt

1 clove garlic, minced

Zest and juice of 1 lemon

3 Tbsp (45 mL) finely chopped fresh dill

Pinch of salt

Pinch of granulated sugar

Combine all ingredients. Refrigerate in an airtight container.

Lemon Vinaigrette

MAKES ¼ CUP (60 ML)

Every cook needs one good go-to vinaigrette that can be used to dress everything from leafy greens to heartier grain and bean salads. This one never fails. If you don't have a fresh lemon, use 1 Tbsp (15 mL) white wine vinegar, red wine vinegar or balsamic vinegar.

1 clove garlic, finely minced

¼ cup (125 mL) extra-virgin olive oil

1 Tbsp (15 mL) Dijon mustard

Juice of ½ lemon

Pinch of salt

Pinch of pepper

Pinch of granulated sugar

Whisk ingredients together until well blended. Refrigerate in an airtight container.

Mascarpone Cream

MAKES 1 CUP (250 ML)

Smooth, silky mascarpone cheese is a staple in our galley refrigerator. It earns its place due to its versatility, working well in both savoury and sweet dishes. We've mixed it with honey, cream and vanilla to make Mascarpone Cream, a luscious addition to everything from breakfast bread puddings to roasted stone fruit.

1 cup (250 mL) mascarpone cheese (choose a creamy variety)

1 Tbsp (15 mL) liquid honey

2 Tbsp (30 mL) cream

1 tsp (5 mL) vanilla extract

Combine all ingredients using a food processor or an electric mixer. On board, you can use your immersion blender. Refrigerate in an airtight container.

Smoked Paprika Aioli

MAKES 1 CUP (250 ML)

This spread is an excellent condiment with everything from Polenta Fries (page 108) to sandwiches and burgers.

1 cup (250 mL) mayonnaise
1 tsp (5 mL) smoked paprika
Juice of ½ lemon
Pinch of salt
1 tsp (5 mL) liquid honey

Mix all ingredients until well combined. Refrigerate in an airtight container.

Wild Blackberry Preserve

MAKES 3 CUPS (710 ML)

In the heat of summer, wild blackberries are plentiful on the back roads of Vancouver Island and the Gulf Islands. Picking this luscious fruit during wanders ashore is an annual pastime for many boaters. The plump, ripe berries are wonderful eaten out of the hand, piled atop granola and yogurt, or baked into a pie. Our family has fond memories of foraging from the tangle of bushes on Hornby Island every summer. We knew the holiday had begun after the first batch of blackberry preserve came off the stove. Breakfasts were not complete without this homemade jam smeared on toasted bread from the Cardboard House Bakery, an island institution.

Keeping a small quantity of granulated sugar and a lemon on board is all that is needed to make blackberry jam on your journey. Make a small batch and eat it fresh. The tart lemon juice cuts through the sweetness. If you have an overstock of apricots, peaches, strawberries or raspberries that have ripened too quickly, consider turning them into a batch of jam, as well. Be adventuresome and experiment with the flavour by adding spices such as cinnamon or cardamom.

2 cups (475 mL) blackberries, crushed

1½ cups (350 mL) granulated sugar

1½ tsp (7.5 mL) lemon juice

In a saucepan over medium-high heat, combine blackberries, sugar and lemon juice. Bring to a boil, then reduce to medium heat. Cook for 10 to 15 minutes until the jam begins to thicken. Skim off foam and allow to cool. Refrigerate in an airtight container.

Resources

FOOD PRODUCERS

In addition to the grocery store chains mentioned in our producer profiles, many of the featured products are available in independent shops, at farmers' markets and on island restaurant menus. For more information on where these products are sold, please visit the websites below or search for the suppliers online.

- Eatmore Sprouts & Greens (www.eatmoresprouts.com)
- Fanny Bay Oysters (www.fannybayoysters.com)
- Foote's Hazelnut Farm (no website)
- Fredrich's Honey (www.fredrichshoney.com)
- Hardy Buoys Smoked Fish (www.hardybuoys.com)
- Hilary's Cheese (www.hilarycheese.com)
- Island Scallops (www.islandscallops.com)
- Island Sea Farms (www.saltspringislandmussels.com)
- Mac's Oysters Ltd. (www.macsoysters.com)
- Nanoose Edibles Organic Farm (no website)
- Ravenstone Farm Charcuterie (www.ravenstonesheepfarm.com)
- Ruby Red Farms (www.rubyredfarms.com)
- Ruckle Heritage Farm (www.ruckleheritagefarm.com)
- Salt Spring Island Cheese Company (www.saltspringcheese.com)
- Saturna Island Family Estate Winery (www.saturnavineyards.com)
- Sea Cider Farm & Ciderhouse (www.seacider.ca)
- True Grain Bread (www.truegrain.ca)
- Untamed Feast (www.untamedfeast.com)
- Vancouver Island Brewery (www.vanislandbrewery.com)
- Vancouver Island Salt Co. (www.visaltco.com)

OTHER RESOURCES

The farmers, growers, fishermen, fine-food artisans and beverage producers profiled in these pages are just the tip of the iceberg in terms of what Vancouver Island and the Gulf Islands have to offer. Prior to departing on your next boating adventure, we encourage you to visit the websites below to uncover information about the culinary points of interest located at or near your destinations.

- For a full listing of the islands' farms, u-pick farms and farmers' markets, please visit Island Farm Fresh at www.islandfarmfresh.com.
- For a full listing of the islands' wineries, cideries, meaderies and distilleries, please visit the Wine Islands Vintners Association at www.wineislands.ca.
- For a listing of British Columbia's craft breweries, please visit the Craft Brewers Association of British Columbia at www.bccraftbeer.com.
- For information on the sustainable seafood choices available in our West Coast waters, please visit Ocean Wise at www.oceanwise.ca.
- For information on fishing regulations and closures, please visit Fisheries and Oceans Canada at www.dfo-mpo.gc.ca.
- For more information on fishing regulations in BC, please visit the Sport Fishing Institute of British Columbia at www.sportfishing.bc.ca.
- For more general information on fishing in BC, and to purchase your fishing licence online, please visit Discover Fishing BC at www.discoverfishingbc.ca.

Acknowledgements

We would like to say thank you to the following individuals for their contributions to *Sea Salt: Recipes from the West Coast Galley*:

To Bill (Lorna's husband and Alison and Hilary's dad), for your encouragement and enthusiasm. Your nautical expertise and knowledge of the Vancouver Island boating region have been invaluable to this project.

To our dedicated taste testers, Ryan Eathorne and Sean Stewart.

To the Harbour Publishing team for believing in this project.

To our photographer, Christina Symons, for brilliantly translating our vision into a reality.

To our editor, Pam Robertson, for the superb work you put into our manuscript.

To Bill and Eleanor Sinclair, for welcoming us into your beautiful garden.

To fellow sailors Julie Beauregard-Stewart, Doug Stewart, Pat Mahoney, Mike Pepler and Tessa and Stu Kenning, for sharing your stunning boating photography with us.

Index

About the Authors

Alison Malone Eathorne (centre) holds a Bachelor of Arts from the University of Western Ontario, a Master of Arts from Griffith University in Brisbane, Australia, and a Bachelor of Education from Vancouver Island University. She has a professional background in writing, editing and communications with a focus on travel, food and interior design. Alison has contributed to *Western Living, BC Home, Vancouver View, Where Vancouver, Where Whistler, Journeys West, Appeal, TV Week* and *BC Business*.

Hilary Malone (right) is a student of Vancouver Island University's Culinary Arts program and holds a Bachelor of Arts from the University of Victoria. The fearless cook in our family, she has demonstrated her mastery of the kitchen in roles as a special events cook and a catering cook. A longtime recipe contributor to *Vancouver View*, she has a keen eye for food photography and styling. Hilary has parlayed her passion for agriculture into planting an extensive organic vegetable garden.

Lorna Malone (left) has a Bachelor of Arts from the University of Western Ontario and is a former teacher, community volunteer and event coordinator. Her passions include sailing, cuisine and horticulture. Lorna's many cruising and racing adventures—including those where she has cooked for eight sailors in a compact galley—have fostered her extensive knowledge of boating in this region and have inspired her to cook with island ingredients.